G000256850

MIS
ORGAN
MAN

Cover: 'Firefly,' 'Prince' and 'Ceōl.'

MISTER ORGAN MAN

LEONARD BROOKS

HERITAGE
HOUSE

MISTER ORGAN MAN

First published August 1994
ISBN 1.85215.1404
Typeset by Chapel Phototypesetting, Ipswich
Printed by Colorcraft, Hong Kong
Published by Heritage House (Publishers) Ltd, 5 King's Road,
Clacton-on-Sea, CO15 1BG

© Leonard Brooks, 1994

CHIAPPA Ltd
31 Eyre Street Hill,
LONDON EC1R 5ET

We are still cutting traditional music for
KEY and KEYLESS ORGANS: 20/30, 46/48, 65, 89/98.

All cutting carried out under the personal care of
ALBERT CHIAPPA.

List on application.

CONTENTS

FOREWORD

FAIRGROUND ORGANS HAVE all but disappeared from the fairground but many, with a sort of wanderlust, still appear at rallies and on our streets. These are the ones that are carrying on the tradition and *Ceōl* is one of them. Leonard, in his book, faithfully describes his adventures with *Ceōl* over the years, with the humour, worry and heartache that go with the problems of trailing an organ around the country, simply for the enjoyment of his listeners.

But not quite. *Ceōl* has collected a small fortune for charity which, in the end, makes it all worth while.

In its way, Leonard's story is typical of the organ owners who use their music-making for the benefit of others — but, unlike them, he has taken the trouble to record the trials and tribulations involved so that we have here in this remarkable little book, an eye-opening story of what goes on behind the scenes. Read this story and you will never again take the travelling organ for granted.

Felix Gameson, F.O.P.S.

1: BAPTISM OF STEAM

LET ME TELL YOU A STORY.

I'm an old man now, well into my eighties, with my sight fading and my hearing propped up by one of those little things in my ear. But as I sit here in the sunshine I so very often think back to the busy life I led until quite recently.

I'm Leonard Brooks. Never heard of me? Then that shows you don't belong to that ever-growing army of people who go around the steam-engine and fairground rallies all summer long.

But maybe you have heard of me? Len — the man who took *Ceōl*, the restored fairground organ, around the country in the sixties and seventies, and well into the eighties. I travelled from Aberdeen to Cornwall, sometimes away from home for several weeks at a time. I was invited on BBC Television's *Playschool* more than once, with *Ceōl*, of course; over the years I rubbed shoulders with plenty of famous people, from politicians to showbusiness personalities. And in the process *Ceōl* and I raised £120,000 for charity — now there's a sum not to be missed!

So that's me; but you'll learn plenty more about me as my story progresses.

Can you imagine life in Britain in the 1920s, when I was a boy, beginning to find out what the world was all about? It wasn't easy. The country was recovering from the savagery of the Great War, and people were beginning to rediscover their simple amusements and pastimes. No radio, of course. No television. The cinema, sometimes miles away, reigned supreme although the films were silent, jerky, either grey or sepia, and frequently snapped during screening.

No wonder it was a time for rejoicing when the travelling fairground came to town.

The first we children knew of the fair's coming was when the showbills were posted up all around town. Then came the first of

7

the caravans — big timber-built trucks on enormous wheels, with brass lanterns and large water churns adorning their outsides. That was when the children shouted "Fair's here!" and, as soon as school was over at 4pm, we rushed to the meadow.

I was fascinated by the gradual build-up, particularly when the first traction-engine arrived. Oh, God! Those big, fiery monsters, handled with such dextrous skill! How wonderful it would be to drive one when I grew up, I thought: not for me the usual boyhood dreams of handling a steam engine confined to railway tracks.

The real treat came on the day the fair opened. I was always there early, before they had even raised steam on the engine. I remember one fair in particular, and an elderly gentleman sitting outside his caravan. They said he was Colonel Print, the boss, but I could never see why a fairground owner should be a colonel: they belonged on the parade ground with rows of medals on their chests. I don't think it was his baptismal name, because there was a lovely old round-about with beautiful lettering on the rounding board, proclaiming it to be "John Print's stud of leaping horses and flying cockerels."

Would you believe, this old ride is still around in the 1990s: I last heard of it in Felixstowe.

But back to my boyhood. The traction engine, properly called a showman's road locomotive, was standing at the edge of the fair, big and green, gently hissing steam and eager for work. If I can recollect correctly, it was the *Victorious*, a proud name for such a mighty beast.

Elsewhere in the fair, I watched a man light the fire in the boiler of a big roundabout — yes, even the roundabouts had their own steam engines — by dropping a piece of flaming oily rag onto a pile of kindling wood. This simple trick which I learned as a lad, was the method I would use years later on my own steam engines.

By around 5pm small boys used to get hungry. Ten minutes later I was home for tea, bursting with almost-suppressed excitement until I could hurry back to the fair, with a warning from mother about not getting into mischief.

Now I could hear the strident notes of the roundabout organ, soon settling down into a rendering of *Light Cavalry*, a glorious tune ideally suited to the motion of the galloping horses on the roundabout.

In the evenings the fairground was always crowded, the bigger lads trying their luck on the coconut shies, the darts and the skittles. Those skittles never ceased to amaze me, and well do I remember the old lady in charge, much older than my granny, and her shouting: "Oh, dear, oh, law! Three out of four!" She would back that up with "One touch and over they go!" — but did they? Those small wooden balls would bounce off the iron skittles without causing a shudder.

But I hadn't time for the sideshows. I was more interested in the roundabout and the steam engine that drove it. There it was, all polished copper and brass, gleaming in the setting sunlight. The man who controlled the engine looked so important as he gently moved the regulator wheel and occasionally stoked a small shovel of coke into the boiler.

I also noticed that he counted the number of riders, and kept an eye on the boys who collected the fares and passed the money to him; my friend, who was quite worldly for his age, told me about 'sticky fingers'.

At that early stage I didn't know the roundabout makers' names, but on thinking about it now, this was probably an eighty-nine key, it was so loud and clear. It was certainly the time I first fell in love — not with a girl, but with a fairground organ.

Then I would move on to admire the big green showman's locomotive being steamed up. This one had a long extension chimney fitted, from which the smoke gently puffed out, and there was a wide belt from the enormous flywheel to a small pulley on the dynamo, which was bolted to a bracket on the smoke box.

I would stand there enthralled by the sight of such power, the whole thing just ticking over, the governors spinning, and the belt clicking rhythmically as its join came around, creating just enough power for the electric bulbs to glow a dull red.

And then, when the sun set, the engine driver opened the fire doors and fed coal into the furnace, as though he knew he was giving all his spectators a splendid performance. Then came the moment we were all waiting for; he gently tapped the regulator open, the engine settled to a steady throb, the pace of the clicking belt increased, and the bulbs went from dull red to dazzling brilliance.

It was wonderful, particularly when scarcely any of us lads had the marvel of electricity in our homes.

When it was quite dark I went back to the steam-driven roundabout and saw a similar magical transformation had happened. The whole fair was ablaze with electric light, scintillating and reflecting off the twisted brass rods of the carousel and off anything else that moved. I stood there, a child lost in wonderland. I would have loved to drive that roundabout, although I expected I would have to start at the bottom, like the boy feeding cardboard music into the fairground organ.

As it happened, in years to come I was to feed hundreds of sheets of music into fairground organs, and I never once got to drive a carousel. Such is life.

My daydreams were shattered when somebody tapped me on the shoulder. Mother, father, and my sisters had come to savour the fun of the fair. They wanted me to join them but I told them I wanted to stay there and listen to the organ.

Mother didn't share my enthusiasm. I remember she said "I don't know how you can stand there all the time, listening to those things and those sooty engines." I suppose mums are not always right.

On Tuesday, the fair moved on, much to the regret of us schoolboys. We had to wait a whole year for its return: summer holidays, Christmas, Easter — but when Print's Fair came back that following year it had Bolesworth's Fair as travelling companion. Now, while

'General Gough,' drawn by Leonard's grand-daughter Teresa Wall.

10

Print's was more of a bucolic set-up for travelling around the Essex circuit, Bolesworth's was sophisticated. It included scenic gondolas, chair-o-planes, a joywheel, and the famous incredible steam yachts.

The gondolas were steam-driven and, before firing up on opening day, Mr Bolesworth called three of us lads over and ordered: "Boys, get a pail each, fill that tank up, and you're all on a free ride." It meant bailing water from the nearby stream, which the fairground people had already dammed, but we were delighted to oblige. In retrospect I reckon that tank held 300 gallons, enough to satisfy the engine's thirst for the entire night.

We got our free ride, tried to stay aboard for another, but Mr Bolesworth was ready. "Come on, now: one ride only, and you've had it."

There was a lovely organ on Bolesworth's gondolas. I'm sure the first tune I recognised was *Three O'clock In The Morning*, which must have been the popular song of the times. And as there was a smaller organ on the steam yachts, there was no lack of music at the fair.

Now, I told you I'd already fallen in love with the fairground organ, but here came a rival for my affections. Her name — or maybe I should say *his* name, was *General Gough*, and he was an absolutely splendid showman's road locomotive from the Burrell works. In the fading daylight the General was a beautiful monster, ticking over gently as it waited for darkness when it would flex its mighty iron muscles and generate electricity for the entire Bolesworth part of the fair. In the daylight I could see its name painted in rich maroon, outlined in gold leaf, so smart it looked as if it had just come from the makers. When the lights went up I noticed the General had a full set of canopy lamps, and something that I have never seen in all the years since: all the bulbs had opaque shades, a crinkled rim of glass around each one.

I would have loved to go up on the footplate, but I had to wait 65 years for that boyhood dream to come true.

Back then in the twenties, I was mentally comparing the Burrell engine and Print's steam engine. They were both doing the same job, but they were in different worlds. The *Victorious* was a hard-working old-timer even then, with no fancy brasswork, and iron rods to support its roof. I was to learn, many years later, that each owner puts something of himself into his steam engine, and *General*

Gough reflected a little bit of Mr Bolesworth.

This time, when the fair moved on, the aura of the fairground organ and the steam engines stayed behind. I was so engrossed in my love that I spent a lot of time in the library, studying the many books on steam and electrical engineering. Already I knew what I wanted to do in life — but actually getting around to doing it was to prove a different matter.

ABOUT THIS TIME London County Council decided to burst its bounds and invade our part of Essex. It was to build a vast housing complex, originally known as the Becontree Estate, but it grew and grew until it swallowed the little village of Dagenham, when the whole seething mass took on the name, and Dagenham was reborn as a large town.

The project was vast. The first big development was the laying of the railway track from the Great Eastern line at Chadwell Heath, to supply the building materials — sand, gravel, cement, bricks, timber, tarmac — for the roads, the houses, the shops. The first we boys knew of it was the track being laid across open farmland, then some days later a locomotive was standing there, much to our delight. I recall precisely that it was a maroon saddle-tank 0-4-0 named *Bombay*, and it looked fairly old.

Of course, we clambered all over it, but found the levers and cocks and other moving parts were covered with thick black grease, a pretty good deterrent for small boys with itchy fingers and a common precaution with the drivers of the steam plough engines.

You remember the steam ploughs? There was a traction engine each side of the field, and they used to haul a set of reversible ploughs from one side to the other on steel cables, moving along a few feet each time.

On the following Sunday we went back to see *Bombay* and the big boys soon had it stoked with hay and lit up. They worked hard feeding hay into the fire and soon a dense cloud of smoke was rising from the funnel. They would never raise steam, I told my pals; they needed lots of coal for that, but within minutes the smoke had attracted the attention of a watchman who came running across the fields blasting on his whistle. I don't remember seeing boys run so quickly.

We were to see *Bombay* steamed up several times after that, as the track extended across the open land, and they built a big engine shed, a sort of temporary construction, probably to keep inquisitive boys off the footplate. There were other things happening in Becontree; steam cranes came in to dig sand and gravel pits, their giant grabs fascinating us as we saw tons of ballast being tipped into the railway trucks. You wouldn't be surprised to know that I can even remember that the biggest crane was built by Thomas Smith of Leeds; it was a fascinating machine to watch as it was self-propelled, ran on standard gauge railway tracks, and could even haul and shunt trucks.

Of course, you have to see things in the perspective of the 1920s. There were no big lorries on the roads, and the few small ones were subject to a maximum speed of 20 miles an hour, not such a bad thing when you consider the state of many of the highways. The traction engine was king of the road, but incapable of anything like that speed. So the railways ruled. Most heavy goods travelled by rail — canals and coastal shipping were the only rivals — and almost every town in Britain was on the rail network. So why should Becontree be any different?

After *Bombay* we had more steam locos: I remember *Lord Mayor, Frances, Somerton, Swansea* and *Partington*, and there were unnamed portable steam engines to power the sawmills, water pumps, and even a 'steam navvy', a massive crane-like giant reputed to have worked on the construction of the Panama Canal; built in Ohio, USA, it scooped huge gobs of soil at each thrust.

Later the steam rollers came to finish off the roads, and brought me my first encounter with temptation at the gullible age of twelve. It happened that, after watching the driver pulling and pushing his levers, I said to two of my young pals: "How about us starting that roller this evening after the men have knocked off?"

When we came back the roller was sheeted over, and an iron plate, weighted down with a brick, was on top of the chimney; this was to keep the fire smouldering and save firing-up time the next day. We couldn't climb to reach this plate so we poked it off with a stick; then we untied a couple of ropes to let me clamber up onto the footplate. My less-adventurous pals stayed on the ground, but with strict orders to keep a lookout for watchmen and coppers.

Up there under that green tarpaulin the footplate was dark and eerie, but so very exciting. It was my first time alone on a steam engine, and the pity of it was that it was on a steam roller and not aboard *General Gough.*

I opened the fire door and saw the flames were bright with the iron plate gone from the chimney top: I didn't give a thought to the driver who would have to relight the fire in the morning.

Now for action. My fingers tingled with excitement as I clutched the heavy reversing lever, left in the midway 'neutral' position when the engine was idle. I pushed it forward. Then I grasped the regulator and gently moved it open, feeling the thrill of the big flywheel beginning to turn, rubbing itself against the tarpaulin.

I then pulled the reversing lever backwards, towards me, and sure enough, the flywheel stopped, then went into reverse. Encouraged by this initial success I opened the throttle a little more; this made the engine start to vibrate, and the exhaust roared, alerting the watchman some way off. Unaware that retribution was on the way, I shut everything down and clambered out from under that sheet, well satisfied with my performance.

"You got her going," my pal Scottie exclaimed. "Can you get her rolling?"

"I reckon so," I lied, but didn't want to confess I had no idea how to put it in cog — in gear, in layman's language. I was spared being put to the test as we saw the watchman running towards us, forcing us to make a hasty retreat.

I revelled in the instant fame at school as word spread around about my exploits — but not reaching the teachers' ears. I now wanted to try something different and soon I noticed a Foden steam wagon was often left in an open yard.

I took my pals back on a Saturday, just after the men had packed up at midday and gone to the *Royal Oak* for liquid refreshment. We used the same technique as with the steam roller: my pals stood guard while I clambered up under the sheet. I had plans to get the engine running in neutral and working the pump and injector, but I didn't want to put the thing in motion.

So much for my plans.

Getting on the footplate was child's play. The engine was hot and sizzling, and there was that pleasing smell associated with all steam engines. The pressure gauge was down to about 60 psi, quite low for a Foden, but enough to play with. The flywheel and reversing

14

lever were much smaller than on the roller, and the regulator was different, and a steel pin locked it in the stop position. I should have paid more attention to that pin before I started playing with the controls: that lapse could have altered my future beyond all recognition.

Full of the confidence born of ignorance, I pushed the reversing lever forward, pulled the pin out of the regulator and left it dangling on a short chain. I pushed the regulator forward — and nothing happened.

I pushed it a bit further and the wagon began to move forward. Suddenly I was scared: I hadn't intended driving the thing. I pulled the regulator right back — and the wagon moved forward even faster. Scottie and Alfie, the lookouts, were shouting at me: "*Mind the wall!*"

In panic, and by pure luck, I found the regulator stop position and thrust the pin back in. But now in terror I slithered from under the tarpaulin and the three of us ran as if all the devils in Hell were after us. One thought was in the front of my mind: *bad boys are sent to reform school.* Reform school was like a prison for children, and the mere thought of being sent there was a great deterrent to most of us. Being naughty, adventurous, mischievous, was all part of being a boy — but being a *bad* boy was something altogether different.

Once I had recovered from the scare, this little incident didn't diminish my interest in steam, and with so much steam machinery around the temptations were great for small boys. I just had to meddle — as on the day when the men had put the locomotives in the shed and I had the uncontrollable urge to pip the whistle on *Frances.* I stealthily climbed onto the footplate and went for the brass handle. It should have just given a brief *pippp!* — but the wretched thing stuck! It was panic all over again, and we just had to run. My pals had a good start, but by the time I was off the loco I could see the watchman's face, and he didn't look pleased.

It turned into an obstacle race; off the site and over the road (impossible in today's heavy traffic); he was following so I skidded into the park with something like a 20-yard lead. But here I had the advantage: I knew a place to jump the brook, where we school lads had done it many times already. I made it, but the man stopped, hurling us a string of expletives as I made my getaway and joined up with Scottie and Alfie. While we caught our breath we realised the engine's whistle was still blowing.

I didn't learn; I was still into mischief with steam whenever I had the chance. The next episode was with a portable steam engine in the sawmill, not far from our last exploit. Now this engine provided the steam which blew the works whistle, telling the men when to start and stop their shift, and it was audible for miles. The whistle was on top of a steel pipe above the sawmill roof and operated by pulling a cord. Our aim was to get to that cord, but we had no means of climbing. Eventually we found a long piece of quartering — timber — but two of us had to manipulate it because of its weight. We couldn't grip the cord so finally we pulled down on the whistle lever.

We got a piercingly loud blast, lovely music to our youthful ears, but we couldn't stand around to enjoy it, could we? Immediately Alfie cried: "*Watchman!*" so we dropped the wood and ran. The watchman gave several long blasts on his own pocket whistle, which probably scared us more than if he'd chased us — and we heard it above the noise of the factory whistle.

Over the years the estate expanded enough to warrant a visit from the fair, so I was able to see *General Gough* and Print's showman's engines again, and I would still have loved to have driven one, but it is better to do one thing than dream all things.

I was growing up quickly now and, rather surprisingly, joined a boxing club, which possibly curbed some of my exuberance. Later, I left school and worked in an electrical laboratory; I think I got the job because my boss was impressed by my interest in steam and model engineering. He was a competent model engineer, his hobby being the building of steam-boats, but he was also a skilled artificer in metals and he taught me how to silver solder, to braze and weld. I learned a lot about electricity, motors and generators from him, but most of all I learned model-making, and I found the riveting of copper boilers particularly fascinating.

The fairs came and went, and my love of engines and organs was undiminished, but at the age of sixteen a boy's thoughts turn to other things. No — not that! I mean motor bikes. And they needed money, not only to buy but to run, and was there ever a time in my youth when money wasn't tight? So I decided to use my boxing talents to fund my motor bike urge.

2: AMBITIONS REALISED

I WAS A GULLIBLE YOUTH — but I suppose almost all my school-mates could have fallen for the same trick. I actually believed that everything I saw in print was true, and that a poster proclaiming a purse of up to £250 for the winner of an amateur boxing contest, meant just that: that there was the equivalent of five years' wages just waiting to be picked up.

I was quite a good boxer, in one of the lower weights, and I saw no reason why I shouldn't earn that purse in one good, clean, honest contest. So I got into the fight game. I won my first contest and received the grand sum of £3, trivial compared with that tempting £250, but it represented three weeks work where I was learning chemical and electrical engineering.

I continued to fight in my spare time until I achieved my first ambition of earning enough to buy a motor cycle. That spurred me into greater things, and I fought until I could buy a brand new Austin Seven car — a 'Tin Lizzie' — which made me the envy of all the boys for streets around.

On form I should have won my next fight, but I broke a thumb and sustained such a bad cut over one eye that the referee stopped the contest. To make bad matters worse, I soon contracted a stitch abscess in the thumb.

Now I couldn't work, and I couldn't fight either. My father suggested I start up in business on my own account, with some help and guidance from him. "And if it succeeds, son, take a tip from me: don't risk it by going back into the ring."

I knew something of basic chemistry and father was in the paint trade, so I decided to make paint. Sadly, the lure of the ring lingered on. I made a comeback in which I lost two fights and drew the third which I thought I had won. It was enough. At last the enthusiasm was gone and at the age of 21 I retired from the ring.

I threw all my energies into the manufacture and sale of paint, which was easy in the days before the industrial giants dominated the scene. I even promised myself that I would have a Rolls Royce by the time I was 40. I didn't — I was in fact 42 when I bought my dream car, which had begun life as the first Rolls to have been sold in Romford. The year was 1952 and the registration was SPU 1. Ironically, nowadays the registration alone would sell for at least £30,000, four times the original cost of the car.

THE OLD ROAD Paint Works prospered in the years leading up to the Second World War, but it grew stronger during the war itself. I knew something about air compressors and the new technique of paint spraying, and taught myself enough to develop that line of business; I even wrote a book, *Car and Industrial Spraying*, which sold nearly half a million copies. It was a best-seller before the term had been invented.

With literary success behind me I started to sell cellulose paint for industrial use and vehicle finishing then, with my father's help, I began manufacturing cellulose spray. We developed a pebble mill — a drum with well-rounded stones — for grinding the pigments to a dust, and got a licence for storing cellulose, a highly flammable substance which we kept in underground tanks.

The Old Road Paint Works was right beside Harold Wood Railway Station, and by a special agreement with the company, later British Railways, we used the station lavatory instead of our own. But we were one of the railway's biggest industrial customers and we would load scores of cans of paint on the platform for distribution all over the country. Thanks to the advertising which the book generated, we were also trading in carriage paint, marine finish, polyester resin filler and, towards the end, emulsion paint.

But I mustn't forget to mention the great event of 1949 when I married, at the age of 40. Doris, who prefers to be called Dee, has been my wife, friend and companion ever since.

Paint may have been bringing me my bread and butter, but steam was still the luxury missing from my daily diet. And then I glanced at the daily paper and saw a story about two men who were going to race their traction engines, with a quantity of beer as the prize.

I would have loved to have seen the event. The very knowledge that steam locomotives were still out there, somewhere, rekindled

Lesley Brooks and 'Prince'; note the driving belt and the chimney extension.

that spark that was still glimmering in my soul, and it would not take much to fan it into the blazing ambition that I had had as a boy.

Soon the talk was of founding clubs for people with traction engines. I had no idea of where these clubs were, or whether I could join. And as there were no books on the subject, I didn't know where to go for the information. I just waited to see what would turn up.

It was Reg Smith, one of our customers, a plant-hire contractor from Inworth, between Chelmsford and Colchester, who turned up, and he had a request for advice on paint for . . . would you believe it, a traction engine! I spent a lot of time with Reg, plying him with questions about traction engine clubs and absorbing all his answers: apparently owners were banding together all over the country, and Reg was now one of that happy breed.

"Come on down on Sunday," he added. "We're steaming her up."

I arrived at Inworth on the Sunday morning in time to see Reg getting up steam on *Empress*, a beautiful tractor built by Richard Garrett Engineering of Leiston, Suffolk: the firm closed in 1980 and the factory is now the Long Shop Museum.

I shan't go into details of the delights of that morning when, for the first time in my life, I was not only allowed to touch the controls, but was actually made welcome.

But the day was also memorable for something else. Not only was I meeting Reg on the social level, but I met his son John for the first time. John, who lived and worked with his father, lent me a booklet by John Crawley on how he had restored the Fowler showman's locomotive *Kitchener*, which in later years was to be renamed *Iron Maiden* and star in the film of that title. John and I were to be friends for life, and I came away from that day at Inworth with a cluster of club booklets, and that inner spark of ambition burning bright, as bright and as powerful as the furnace in *General Gough* at Bolesworth's fair all those years ago.

I was hooked on steam, and this time it would stay with me for the rest of my days.

But life had changed. Now a full-grown man, I was able to go out and buy a steam engine of my own. Reg's advice had been prudent: 'Make haste slowly,' and he had suggested that I go to some of the rallies and make a steam roller my first investment: I could probably buy one for a hundred pounds.

Now, £100 may not sound much but in 1963 it was worth the equivalent of several thousand pounds in the nineties. Even so, steam engines were cheap: what £100 bought you then, £10,000 would not buy you today. Even so, I said "No." I didn't want a road roller; I wanted a showman's road locomotive, something like *General Gough*, but he, of course, would scarcely have survived the past forty years and the Second World War. Nonetheless, I was going to start at the top of the ladder, not somewhere down near the bottom.

The quest for a boiler-tested engine was proving very difficult until I saw an advertisement in a newspaper to which Reg and John Smith had introduced me: *World's Fair*. Of course, today's steam buffs know that *World's Fair* is of second importance only to the Highway Code (or should I also include the Bible?) but the non-indoctrinated reader must understand that this is a weekly newspaper aimed at showmen, preservationists and market traders.

The advert offered a Burrell agricultural engine in first class condition, and a phone call revealed that it belonged to Walter Rasberry of Grimston, near King's Lynn in Norfolk. I had quite a long chat with Walter who finally suggested that I come to see the engine the next morning, a Sunday.

When I arrived I found Walter's home, and his steam engine, were beside his motor service station in the village. Walter and I took to each other at once and soon he invited me into his large workshop, well equipped with tools and machinery, including a useful lathe.

"There she is," Walter said, waving his hand to an immaculately-kept engine, unique in not having a name: she was just number 4037.

I stood spellbound, admiring her with the knowledge that in an hour or so 4037 could be mine. Then came the surprise.

Walter said: "I'll back her out into the yard so you can have a good look around." I hadn't even realised that 4037 had steam up, as there was no hiss, no crackle, no drip of water, and no smoke. Walter certainly knew his steam engines.

When we had 4037 out in the daylight I could see that she was in superb condition, especially the gears; in fact the engine showed very little sign of use. There would certainly be no heavy restoration to do, but as 4037 was just an agricultural traction engine and not a showman's road engine, she could never be a *General Gough*. Despite that, I found myself saying, with a lump in my throat: "I'll have her."

And so the boy in Chadwell Heath who had dared to drive a Foden steam lorry and nearly smashed a wall, became the man who, forty years later, bought his own steam engine. It had been a long road — but the real journey was only just beginning.

A FEW DAYS LATER a low-loader brought 4037 to Harold Wood. As quickly as possible I had a shed built, large enough for a showman's road locomotive and not just an agricultural tractor. The next step was to park 4037 in her new home. I thought about this a lot; it involved raising steam for the first time, reversing in a wide sweeping manoeuvre around two storesheds and a pair of solvent pumps, and bringing the engine's tender near the main gates, before going forward into the new shed. It was the moment of truth for me: was I to do it myself, or get someone more experienced to help? Despite the risks, which I didn't want to think about, I decided to do it all myself, on a Sunday.

On the chosen day I removed the sheets, clambered onto the footplate to check the water, then put plenty of wood in the firebox and lit it with a rag dipped in oily waste. Soon I piled in the coal but, remembering the advice to keep the fire thin, I didn't put in enough. Two hours later and with no pressure registering on the gauge, I realised that I could see the fire bars. I added more coal and half an hour later there was enough pressure for me to start.

Ah! One of the greatest days of my life! My very own engine, and I was going to drive her! I put her in low gear, pushed the reversing lever forward and very cautiously opened the regulator. 4037 gently moved forward but after about three feet I stopped her. Then came the tricky bit. I pulled the reversing lever back and came backwards a few inches, testing my ability to stop her if necessary. I quickly found that having the reversing lever in mid-position gave me excellent control.

I kept to this stop-start method, constantly checking my progress, and found the turning circle was much less than on a motor car, and so I progressed tender-first towards the gates. All that was needed now was to stop, engage forward gear, and drive into the shed, but back came the ghosts of those exploits as a boy, hiding under the tarpaulin and nearly crashing the Foden into a brick wall.

I was ultra-cautious. I laid an old railway sleeper across the shed floor to prevent me 'doing a Foden' and crashing through the end of the new shed. It was a sensible precaution, but unnecessary as my twenty-yard drive was carried out perfectly, and I brought 4037 to a halt in her new home.

The sad part was that this was the only time I ever drove dear old 4037, and after I sold her I never saw or heard of her again. What happened to her?

Only a few days after I put 4037 in her shed, I was on the phone to George Hawkins of Wadebridge, Cornwall, a well-known traction-engine owner and enthusiast in the south-west. George told me he had a 4hp Fowler showman's engine for sale, and I was tempted; it was a showman's engine I really wanted so I could take it to rallies, generate electricity for a fair organ, and put it to a variety of other uses that were half-formed in my mind.

So I went to Cornwall. Everybody in Wadebridge knew George and his *Firefly*. I liked the engine on sight; she was built in 1917 by John Fowler of Leeds, had a sound boiler and had recently had a new firebox, but she was minus her belly tanks and a few brass embellishments, and she needed to be painted. I thought about her for a few days then decided to buy.

Firefly arrived at the Old Road Paint Works at Harold Wood a week later and stood in the yard, while 4037 occupied the shed. Obviously one would have to go. And so it was that soon after buying 4037 I advertised her in *World's Fair* and the first viewers took her. I was sad to see her leave, almost before I had got to know her, but that was life.

As soon as possible I had *Firefly* towed and pushed into the shed, while I listed the jobs that had to be done on her. As soon as word spread in the community that I was restoring a traction engine, I had a steady supply of offers of help from parts suppliers, engineers, and amateurs willing to do anything; I was pleasantly surprised at the reaction.

The first task was to fit new belly tanks, followed by an injector, a pair of safety valves, two resin-ply fascia boards for the roof, then copper piping to replace the out-of-character iron, new brass nuts and bolts, a variety of electrical fittings . . . It was something like a shopping list that didn't know how to end.

We had the boiler test carried out while the cladding was removed, and it turned out to be little more than a formality, the inspector saying that there would be no problem in letting the full working pressure remain at 200psi.

You'll want to know what work we did on the old *Firefly*? We started by replacing the boiler lagging, and used new wooden slats as the old ones were showing signs of distress. We prepared her for a repaint by taking off her wheels — and when we checked the rubber tyres we found them in perfect condition.

The work went on all that winter of 1966-'67. It was a bonus for me to have the engine in the works, so I could sneak in an hour or two during the day. Soon after Christmas *Firefly* was looking quite a smart showman's engine, particularly with the new signwriting on her canopy, the letters outlined in gold leaf.

Meanwhile, my new friend Claude Jessett, a well-known character in the traction engine world, was casting numerous brass embellishments in his foundry at Hadlow Down on the southern edge of the Kentish Weald, and we also had on order some brass twist as I thought the roof was a trifle unstable. Hadlow Down, by the way, was soon to be a regular call on my itinerary as Claude staged one of the best rallies in the business here.

With spring approaching I thought it time for a steam test and the setting of the new safety valves; we could fill the boiler now as the chance of a freeze-up was negligible. She took fifty gallons, and ninety minutes to raise steam, then we set the new valves. What a difference they made! The old pair was erratic and slow to cut off, but the new ones, on the pop-action principle, were very sharp. There were the usual small weeps, and joints that needed a little packing, but the only big change I thought necessary was to replace the eight-inch dynamo pulley with a four-inch one as the engine had to work too hard to generate the required 110 volts.

A week later the brass castings and twist supports were in place, and the only major step left was the final steam test for the boiler.

And that was where I had a problem. If I could get the inspector out on a Sunday, I would be clear. You see, *Firefly* was housed in a paint works, where cellulose solvents were stored and there was always the likelihood of the petroleum inspector walking in. He knew about the engine, of course, but he had never seen her with steam up. All it needed was for me to have *Firefly* steaming in her shed and the two inspectors meeting face to face. Even though the solvent tanks were underground I could imagine the reaction, and the instant withdrawal of licences. But then, I had already had near-disastrous encounters with steam engines forty years earlier.

The boiler inspector readily agreed to a Sunday test — most engines those days never steamed up at all from Monday to Friday, anyway — and *Firefly* performed well. I wanted to take her on a road test as well, but I thought better of it: the local press was agitating for a story and pictures and I thought I'd better have them there for the first venture out into the great wide world.

I made a date with the Romford *Times* for another Sunday, and we had a glorious day — with just one problem. I drove *Firefly* around the block while the photographer caught the paper's motoring correspondent at the controls; he turned in a brilliant report as if he had been road testing a new model of car, but with more humour. Then I parked the steaming monster on the firm's forecourt for a colour photograph that was to make a postcard advertising our paint products — and a picture on the cover of this book. We had just put the old girl back into her shed when the man who lived next door to the works came to me, looking serious.

"Mr Brooks, we are worried about this traction engine. My wife doesn't feel safe with it being so close to our home."

I tried to reassure him: it was tested, approved, and fully insured.

"But what about the smoke? It'll be terrible when my wife hangs out the washing."

He had a point, poor man. I told him I'd use Welsh steam coal that would keep the problem to a minimum, but added that now the testing was complete we'd be away to rallies with the engine. I hope I settled his worries.

THE PRESS REPORT really started something. Other newspapers picked up the story and soon we were taking bookings for public appearances. The first was impressive indeed — the Easter Parade in London's Battersea Park. It was too far to steam, so we would make our debut into the rally world on a low loader.

The parade was scheduled for Easter Monday so the family spent the Sunday getting *Firefly* ready for her great day. Our daughters Pamela, Lesley and Cheryl did the polishing and brother-in-law Les prepared the low-loader while I laid the fire ready for lighting with an oily rag, and had everything else prepared.

Monday dawned pleasant and sunny, just perfect for our run to London. Les and I backed the low-loader out of the yard and we were away. We had plenty of time and there was little traffic going into east London, but when we reached Bow the main road was closed and diversion signs were everywhere.

The diversion was not too difficult for a start, although it was slow. We were about to congratulate ourselves when we saw a low railway bridge in front of us.

"Damn it!" I snapped. "We'll have to pull well over for this one," I told Les, who was driving.

He stopped, allowing a stream of cars to pass us on this one-way stretch of road. We looked at the problem and decided the only thing possible for us was to approach the tunnel dead in the middle, with me walking ahead to sight the top of *Firefly*'s chimney and the tunnel ceiling. The risk of not making it was unthinkable: even if we could reverse this load down the narrow road, into the oncoming traffic and without a police escort, it would take us the rest of the day.

We held up the cars behind us, eased out into the centre of the road, where the traffic came from both directions, and inched forward. And *Firefly* squeezed through with just about two inches clearance.

From there on the journey was uneventful and we still arrived in good time. But I realised the sober truth that travelling with a steam engine and, later, with a fairground organ, would never be straightforward; on the journey anything could happen and at journey's end we would almost always have an audience of inquisitive, interested, and often very knowledgable people. On this Easter Monday, for example, I was answering all manner of questions as I worked, and I don't know who was the more excited — me, or the spectators pouring in by the hundred and soon by the thousand.

I do know we were in very good company, for one of the most popular vehicles in that parade was the magical car *Chitty Chitty Bang Bang*, the star of the 1968 musical. The film had Dick van Dyke, Sally Ann Howes, Lionel Jeffries, Benny Hill, James Robertson Justice and others among its human cast, and the car upstaged those of them who were there that day. And there was a steam roller in the parade; its owner chided me for, as he put it, 'bath-chairing' *Firefly* on a low loader. But his roller had to come only a few miles.

It was a splendid day. I will never forget that Easter Parade, nor the crowds applauding each entry as it passed, rather like a Mexican wave surges through the spectators at a football match. And as *Firefly* was also advertising *Leonard Brooks Ltd, Harold Wood*, we didn't mind how much applause we received. A photo of the engine appeared in a paint journal with the caption *a great saleslady*, but I must stress that we never entered a rally for money. Usually we would have our expenses paid but otherwise we attended purely for the love of it.

But sometimes that love can be tested to its limits, as when we were driving *Firefly* home on the low-loader. On the approach to Chelsea Bridge a policeman stopped us. "Are you aware, sir, that there's a weight restriction on this bridge?"

I answered in innocence: "I'm sorry. I didn't think it applied to us." I didn't want to have to turn around and navigate through the backstreets of south London, no easy task for two amateurs and a steam engine.

"What does this lot weight?" the policeman asked.

"Just over five tons," I ventured, although I suspected the engine and lorry on the weighbridge would total ten tons.

"It looks well over that to me," he said, but I noticed a softening in his manner.

"We came over the bridge this morning," I said, adding: "We're strangers to London."

The policeman shrugged his shoulders. "Go on then, sir, but if you finish up in the river . . ."

There was just the other matter of the low railway bridge. We left our normal route at Aldgate, headed along the Commercial Road and picked up the A13, a longer route but quite easy.

Did I say easy? There were roadworks on the Barking bypass, forcing through traffic up a steep ramp, giving us the risk of grounding as the road levelled at the top. We had no choice but to take it — and I never did know what our margin of clearance was beneath the trailer. We got home at dusk, utterly exhausted, but we agreed we'd had a splendid day.

The next weekend we took *Firefly* to Enfield, north of London. The show was mainly for vintage vehicles but there were steam engines, rollers and organs. And it was here that I first met two new characters who were to play their separate but important roles in my life.

One was Bert George, who owned a Chiappa organ and a nice Aveling & Porter showman's tractor. The other was Tommy Redburn, who owned *Ceōl*, later to become my own organ. Tommy, who had just brought *Ceōl* back from a successful tour of Ireland, said that as his wife was Irish they often visited the Emerald Isle and it was there he had found the 48 Keyless Chiappa in a bad state of repair in a showman's yard. Tommy had bought it and sent it to Victor Chiappa to rebuild.

We arrived at Enfield on Saturday morning and had *Firefly* in steam for the midday start, as we were going to generate the electricity — 110volts DC — for *Ceōl*, in addition to powering the forty-six 60-watt bulbs fixed around the rim of our canopy. The extra current required for *Ceōl* was a small amount, but I soon learned a vital lesson, that while even a slight reduction in voltage never made any visible difference to the lighting, it certainly affected the organ's performance — the machine played slower and sounded awful.

It was as we left the rally to head home that we had our only collision in all the years we spent on the road. I was driving — that means I was operating the steam controls and moving the machine while Len, the steersman, had the wheel and was in control of where we went. We headed for the low loader, when suddenly Les spun the wheel as fast as he could. It was too late. *Firefly* hit the overhanging tip of a fire-engine's ladder with a terrible crunch. I stopped to investigate, but the ladder was undamaged, the only casualty being our canopy which had one piece of timber shattered, many light bulbs smashed, and some wiring ripped out.

As soon as we were home we began the repairs, as we had a booking in the Streatham Carnival on the following Saturday. The repair was finished by Friday evening, even though we had to force-dry the paintwork.

After Streatham came our first steam rally, at Pirton, a tiny village near Hitchin, Herts. Impresario Johnny Mayes was the promoter, and I remember his prediction that steam events such as this were only in their infancy in the sixties and that in years to come they would develop into major events. How right he was — but what happened to him? After a few more rallies he seemed to disappear.

Pirton was a landmark event. Not only was the cameraderie excellent, with everybody bonded by their love of steam, but I made several friends as well as supplying power for *Ceōl* once again. This was where I met Peter Bish who, I believe, was the first amateur — that is, non-professional — fair organ builder, and the man who started the trend which resulted in the building of many neo-organs. I don't use the term disparagingly, merely to differentiate between a genuine old organ that has been restored, and a new one built in the old style.

It was at Pirton, and at Johnny Mayes's later rallies, that I met other stalwarts of the preservation world, such as Teddy Reed, Norman Woodford, Steve Neville and Phil Ives.

But the most important new contact must surely be Victor Chiappa himself, the virtuoso of the organ world and a man who was to become a close friend over the years.

3: CHIAPPA INTERLUDE

AS VICTOR CHIAPPA was to fair organs what Isaac Newton was to the Law of Gravity, let me interrupt my story to tell you something about the man.

He was born in Clerkenwell, London, on 7 September 1900, when steam power was at the height of its popularity and influence. His grandfather Giuseppe had been an organ builder for the famous Gavioli brothers in Paris, but had brought his entire family to London in 1864 to begin building organs on his own account. He settled in the cottages at numbers six and eight Little Bath Street, in Clerkenwell, now renamed Eyre Street Hill, but stayed only a short while before falling under the spell of the New World and the stories of instant fortunes that could be made there.

They tried America for two years but, as that fortune didn't appear to be on the way, they headed back to London, leaving Victor's uncle Enrico — Harry — behind; Harry became a soldier of fortune and travelled the world.

The most amazing thing about the Chiappa family's return was that they managed to move back into the same cottages in Little Bath Street, which had lain unoccupied for those two years. They started back in business by making barrel organs, which they called pianos as the finished thing looked something like an upright piano but with a crank-handle at one end. The operator mounted his organ on a barrow, turned the handle at a regular speed, and out came music. The secret was in the 'barrel', a metal cylinder with short pins on it, which plucked metal reeds; the idea survives today in the musical box.

Chiappa expanded quickly and was soon acting as London agent for the Gavioli brothers in Paris, as well as moving into the building and repair of fair organs. These machines operated on a different principle as their music came from a 'book' of card pages with holes punched at the right places: air pumped through the holes operated valves which allowed other air under higher pressure to play the appropriate notes on the reeds of wind-operated organs such as you see in churches. The cards didn't feed the pipes directly. Business was doing well and soon the firm had 40 workers.

Around this time Giuseppe's son Lodovico — known as Louis — married. Louis, one of the mainsprings of the business, had four children — Albert, Victor, and two daughters.

The Chiappa business was nearly wiped off the face of London in 1912 when one of the buskers who hired barrel organs by the day, brought it back to the Little Bath Street works in the evening, but forgot to take his smouldering pipe out of a small locker. Imagine the scene: a compact factory full of racks of wood, highly flammable polishes, and the finished organs stacked tightly away for the night, as well as other machines in for repair. The fire was well alight before anybody noticed and called the brigade, but the works was saved.

By 1914 the Great War was threatening. Albert was in the factory, doing the highly-skilled job of making the pin barrels. Victor was fourteen and as his father Louis thought he would benefit from an engineering apprenticeship, Victor was packed off to Tylers Ltd in York Way, near King's Cross Station, where he worked on AEC engines and the Ensign car — now, there are names that bring back memories!

Albert enlisted in the King's Own Scottish Borderers, was badly wounded in France and sent back home. The family travelled to see him in Manchester only days before he died.

Victor was conscripted in 1918 into the newly-created Royal Air Force and put to work on aero-engines. After demob he went back to the firm, which was struggling in the post-war era; as there were no finance companies, and banks didn't want to know the small businessman, Victor had to go out to collect cash from the slower-paying customers.

By the 1920s Chiappa Ltd had developed the 'Penny in the Slot' barrel organ, with the fledgling Keith Prowse handling the sales and rentals. The organ business was booming again, with craftsmen builders often working twelve-hour shifts and the six girls, cutting the music books, working ten hours a day. Victor's uncle Charles was in charge of the master cards for mass production, although

A Marenghi organ at the Chiappa works; this organ probably went to the Southend-on-Sea Kursaal.

he suffered from asthma.

Charles Chiappa's music was the best, according to the showmen of the day, and his work is still prominent in the huge library of master copies methodically stored upstairs in the old Chiappa works. I can vouch that Chiappa's card is the most durable as I inherited quite a lot of books with *Ceōl*, and after twenty years of hard work they are still quite sound, while the cards from some other makers didn't last ten years.

Eventually Charles's asthma, exacerbated by the London fogs, grew so bad that he went back to Italy hoping to recover in the warmer climate, but he died of bronchitis. The Chiappas, having lost not only a loved member of family but also a skilled craftsman, turned to the Marenghi Company in Paris, who obliged by releasing Louis Blanche. Louis took over Charles's role and also went out on site to repair organs. He stayed in Britain when Hitler's armies invaded his native France, and would be bombed out of his Wood Green home, but would survive.

The 1930s were difficult years as much of the industrialised world moved into depression, and Victor told me of one incident typical of those hard-up times. A lorry, which had brought an organ from Wales in for repair, would not start when it was due to make the homeward journey. Chiappa's mechanics inspected, and found the bearings were badly worn, but as nobody had the cash for a major repair job, the mechanics packed the bearings with machinery belt, put in fresh oil, and sent the lorry carefully on its way. It got back to Wales — and the organ it carried was the lovely Limonaire that my good friend John Keeley owns today.

Early in the decade, ice skating was popular at the Alexandra Palace, but the band used to stop for short refreshment breaks and so disrupt the evening's enjoyment. When the breaks became too long and frequent, the management sacked the band and called Chiappa's people in to install a massive Marenghi 89-key fair organ, which played until the outbreak of war.

Chiappa eventually bought back the Marenghi, sold the brass to a showman, and left the remainder of the organ standing in the workshop. I first saw it around thirty years later, still gathering dust, and I saw it again in 1992, scarcely touched by the passage of time, except for the dust.

The Chiappa empire began contracting during the depression; the barrel-organ business had gone, showbusiness people were reluctant to speculate, and with the coming of World War Two the fairground business stopped dead.

But the British way of life struck back and, after the shock waves of the phoney war of 1940, a few amusement caterers reopened for limited business. The government later started a Holidays At Home project, intended to give war workers a break from their toils without having to travel to the seaside, and this stimulated fairground interest a little. Chiappa, however, stayed in business almost entirely on the income derived from repairing organs, which was not a lucrative operation in the midst of total war.

And then came the second fire. This time it was no accident; the works were left unoccupied at midday on a Saturday while the few employees went off to lunch. A youth on the prowl wandered in, found some wood shavings, and piled them into heaps, one on the ground floor and another on the first floor. He set fire to them, then ran. He was caught, but the law did little to punish him — rather like some of the over-lenient courts of today — although there was considerable damage done to the factory, with the top floor so badly damaged that it was never rebuilt.

With the end of hostilities in 1945, Chiappa's business began to pick up, but there was another tragedy with the death of Louis Chiappa, leaving his son Victor as the only member of the family in the business.

Slowly, demand for music grew as the fairground organs began to reappear, and most needed major repairs after many years of inactivity and neglect. Louis Blanche was now in poor health, soon to die, leaving Victor with considerable problems as he needed the Frenchman's help with marking the music (preparing the cards for punching) following the loss of several master copies in the fire.

Victor told his troubles to a showman who had recently been demobilised from the Royal Marines, and so heard about James Tiller, a musician and an organ specialist from Long Sutton in Lincolnshire, who had composed a march for the Marines. Victor went to the Fen country and established a relationship with James that was to last a lifetime.

Soon another valuable contact was made. Horace Holmes had been building organs with his father in Manchester, but when Mr Holmes senior retired to the Isle of Man, Horace came south to join

Chiappa. He was a good craftsman, and I remember him working on my organ *Ceól* some years ago. He was around ninety when he died.

The postwar revival of interest in the fairground was short-lived. Like so many other activities it fell victim to the rapid march of television, followed by greater sophistication of the average family, and finally by the electronics invasion and the amusement park. A few fairgrounds survive, and may even be slowly regenerating, but steam power has passed into history and today's roundabouts are plug-in devices designed to hurl the human body in as many directions as possible, all at the same time.

After a period in the doldrums, with the shire horse and old-style farming, interest has revived in steam, in organs, and in anything belonging to the old fairground, but it's no longer the attraction for children and the young-at-heart in a once-yearly visit from the showmen. Now it's a specialist interest for a growing number of steam buffs, amateur engineers and dedicated restorers, and they meet at rallies around the country.

I asked Victor Chiappa a few years ago if he saw a future for fairground organ builders. He paused for thought then said that small builders may cash in on the present interest, but the market is limited as the trade users are almost non-existent.

Talking to Victor, the last in the line of the Chiappa family, it's sad to think that the business founded by his grandfather rose to become a famous name in showland, then declined because of a changing world and the inability to compete. Victor's son Albert, born in 1935, became an organ builder in his own right but in later years had to look upon his skills purely as a hobby, and one of the last major jobs that old Victor did was to make an organ for his grandson's Scout troop. He was like his music: built of strong stuff, but he died in 1992, aged 92.

4: OH, *FIREFLY!*

BUT I DEVIATE. The next few outings with *Firefly* were mostly to carnivals, and the engine proved a great advertisement for the Old Road Paint Works. We drove past big crowds in Romford, Horn-church, Basildon, Southend and Brentwood, and spent several days at a trade exhibition. The engine gave no trouble at all and I was surprised when, at the next boiler test, the inspector said *Firefly* would have to be retubed. I know it's a little bit naughty to say so, but I don't think that inspector knew much about the business.

However, the law had spoken, and a retube it had to be. I discussed it with my friend Jim Russell of Banbury who had a John Fowler *Jemima*, a similar engine to mine. He suggested I bring *Firefly* so the Banbury Traction Engine Club could work on her in Lampitt's

Victor Chiappa (left) and his apprentice Eddie, surname unknown, with the Marenghi organ which went to the Alexandra Palace Skating Rink. Photo taken c 1921.

old yard in the town, where spare tubes were available.

If you've ever dealt with internal combustion engines, I'm sure you know how temperamental they can be — worse than steam engines, I'm sure. Put the two together, and you can appreciate the trouble Les and I had on that journey to Banbury the following Sunday; in its own way it rivalled our adventures on the way to the Battersea Easter Parade. We set out early, with *Firefly* strapped onto the low loader, and we got through the north London suburbs with no problems, but I was well aware of the many people who stared at us as we passed: most were undoubtedly admiring the rare sight, but there were probably a few calculating the scrap value of the brasswork.

Shortly before noon with Banbury not so far away, we stopped for a bite and a coffee, and also to check the map. Soon we noticed more spectators at a farm on the other side of the road, and we swapped questions and answers with them, telling them something about *Firefly* in return for road directions. I must say a traction engine provides a wonderful way to start casual friendships.

But when we went back to the lorry, Les couldn't get her to start. Damnation! Sunday, and miles from base — where do we turn for help? We couldn't abandon the low loader or some enterprising friend would relieve *Firefly* of her brass. We tried all the usual tricks to induce a diesel engine to start, but finally we had to ask our new friends at the farm for a tow with their tractor.

When we met Jim Russell we decided not to switch off the motor, so we left it idling while we unloaded poor *Firefly* by hand winch in unseemly haste. Bidding Jim a quick farewell we set out for home, arriving some time after sunset and still without killing that damned diesel until we were safe in the yard.

Only then did I dare say: "Les, just for the hell of it — try the starter."

He did, and the motor burst into life straight away. And it never ever gave us that problem again.

Three weeks later we went back to Banbury to collect the retubed *Firefly*, but decided not to stop for coffee on the way. When we arrived at Lampitt's works we were pleased to see that Jim had got the traction engine in steam. He gave Les and me a tour of the old works where in bygone years many traction engines had been repaired and, I believe, several had been built. The place was like a museum to the steam era as most of the machinery was belt-driven. Then Mr Lampitt himself came to meet us; he was a venerable gentleman in his nineties, and when he listened to *Firefly* ticking over he remarked: "I think the valve needs moving forward slightly."

ONE DAY WHEN I was talking traction engines to a car breaker, he commented that he had a clapped-out portable steam engine in his meadow. It wasn't his, but he had the owner's authority to make a sale.

"So how much does he want?"

"Hundred and fifty quid. Come over and have a butcher's."

I went two weeks later, cautious not to appear too eager. Sure enough, the engine was a fairly large portable built by Ramsome, Simms & Jeffries of Ipswich, but it certainly was in poor condition. The young man who owned it said he had steamed it up to 20psi but, if that were true, I'm glad I wasn't there at the time.

Now, I don't know why; probably because I didn't want it cut up for scrap, but I offered him a hundred pounds. He turned it down, telling me all the fabulous sums reputed to have been paid for engines. I remained firm, and when I used that time-tried ruse of showing him the money he collapsed, and I was the owner of a beat-up portable which was soon dumped in the corner of our over-filled yard.

I didn't see myself doing anything with it or to it, so I put it up for sale. The response was fair, and I eventually sold it for £150 to a farmer, provided I could transport it a hundred miles.

I knew Les could, even after the breakdown on the way to Banbury. The engine was a heavy old thing to load but Les got it to journey's end with no trouble on the road. However, that's when trouble of another kind happened because that damned farmer sold Les a boat! Now, I know what boats can do to a man — I was nearly hooked on them myself, until steam took over — but it meant I lost Les.

My pal John Smith soon took Les's place, but as I was finding more pleasure in steaming *Firefly* to rallies than in putting her on and off the low loader, I sold the lorry. It meant, of course, that I was confined to travelling much shorter distances.

And then, for no reason I could ever understand, I got the urge to buy a Foden steam wagon. Maybe there was some sort of method in my madness because a Foden would travel faster than *Firefly* and therefore further, and it could carry plenty of coal, water, and miscellaneous items.

A few weeks later I found a 1929 Foden advertised in the pages of *World's Fair*, and travelled over to Wiltshire on a spare Sunday to see it. After a demonstration by its owner, a Mr Chappell, I could see that the engine was in good condition, and the only work needed was on the roof and part of the cab. Mr Chappell had named his beauty *Little Lady*, and he told me something of her story: she had been bought new by Sadd & Co of Maldon, Essex, a firm of timber merchants, for hauling stock around the yard. *Little Lady* was, indeed, a tractor, with a large tank behind the cab.

What undoubtedly struck me most forcibly that day was when Mr Chappell gave me a demonstration run to show me just what a Foden tractor could do. We were driving on a fairly wide open regulator when he said: "If you want extra power for a short spell, here's 'double high'," and he pulled the regulator back sharply, past the 'stop' position. Instantly the engine surged with immense power and the tractor bounded forward. The incident took me back to my boyhood and showed me just how close I had come to crashing that other Foden through a brick wall. I saw now that I could have ended that adventure in hospital, in the mortuary, or in reform school.

Oh, yes. I bought the *Little Lady*.

A WEEK LATER I opened *World's Fair* to see that Tommy Redburn's organ *Ceòl* was for sale.

I pondered. I must admit I was tempted, but did I really want a fair organ? As I had seen it at several rallies I knew it was a smart machine, and had been back to the Chiappa factory for a major overhaul. I compromised by giving Tommy a non-committal ring.

Tommy told me he was selling because he needed the money — poor Tommy was always short of cash — this time to have central heating installed in his public house.

"I'd love you to have it, Leonard. It's a nice organ, built for showland by Chiappa and just been reconditioned by Victor himself. Why don't you come and see it?"

I went over to Enfield, not with the intention of buying, but you can guess what happened. Tommy switched the power on and the air pump began humming gently. He chose one of the 'books' of music, a series of stiff cards mounted in a continuous strip with soft hinges, allowing the whole thing to fold like a concertina. Each card has a series of holes punched in it, and when the book is mounted in its slot in the organ — the keyframe — it is fed through an air gate at a steady but variable speed: the operator can make the music go faster or slower without altering its pitch.

This air in turn operates other valves which allow air from the bellows to vibrate thin strips of metal, called 'reeds' as the original ones were reed leaves, and so produce a musical note. A round hole gives a short *peep!* and a long hole gives a sustained note. Of course, all you fair organ buffs knew that already.

The book that Tommy put on the organ, I shall never know whether by design or accident, was *The Poet and The Peasant*. It sounded magnificent, moreso because it was played under proper acoustic conditions. And that tune sold me the organ.

"Okay, okay, Tommy. I'll buy it. But I just do not know where I'll put it. Any rate, I'll come and collect it next week."

"Now, what in God's name have you done?" I asked myself, and all the way home I told myself the answer. "You've got two steam engines — *Firefly* and *Little Lady* — and even though you've just sold the portable engine in the yard, it doesn't give you any space to store the organ. You're a sentimental old fool, Leonard Brooks, and it's time you stopped this impulse buying. You've just got to face it: something has to go."

The big question was — what?

FIREFLY WAS DOING her rounds of carnivals and fêtes, the next one on her schedule being the Basildon Carnival on August Bank Holiday Monday of 1970.

On the Sunday my daughters Pam, Lesley and Cheryl were busily polishing the brass while I attended to the more important things (*I* think they're more important, but the girls didn't always agree) such as chopping the kindling wood and stacking it in the firebox, topping up *Firefly*'s 90-gallon water tanks, and loading half a hundredweight (25kg) of best steam coal in the tender. I remember moaning about the price: £18 a ton!

With the preparations complete we used the new aquisition, a Series I Land-Rover, to push the old girl back into her shed for the night.

I digress to remind you that a paint works was not the ideal site to cosset a fire-eating monster, and that Harold Wood railway station, still served by steam-driven locomotives, was next to the factory.

I was up at seven on Bank Holiday morning, throwing the blazing oilrag onto the kindling, and wisps of white smoke were seeping out of the joints in the shed roof as I heard a steam train pull up in the station. Almost before I could start putting the coal in, and so dampen the smoke, the phone rang.

"Not today! What a day for somebody to run out of paint!" I decided to let it ring — but then I realised it could be a call from John Smith, who was due to steer for me. I picked up the receiver.

"Is that the paint works? Do you know your shed's on fire? I was just passing in the train and saw the smoke."

I gathered my wits and thanked the caller, assuring him all was under control.

"I'll call the fire brigade if you want," the Samaritan offered.

"No! No, thanks! I can manage! That's okay!" Fire brigade? Firemen were the last visitors I wanted that morning!

As my neighbours were still not keen on having a traction engine parked near their house, and my reputation was growing — after all, *Firefly* advertised the paint works on her canopy — I could guess which of my collection would have to go. But I could worry about that later.

The newly-acquired Land-Rover made an excellent tender; it had an open truck body and I had fitted an A-bar to the front so the vehicle could be towed behind the steam engine with no need for anybody to steer. Now, on this day I decided the Land-Rover would carry two 40-gallon oil drums filled with water, just in case *Firefly* had to drive several miles around town in addition to the 24-mile return trip to Basildon. After all, she did something like six gallons to the mile.

While the hose filled the drums, I loaded spare coal aboard the Land-Rover. Then I noticed a little jet of water coming from midway up one drum. I grumbled until I remembered I had some Sylglas in the shed — it's intended to patch leaks on greenhouse roofs, but it made an excellent repair to the outside of that drum, and resisted the water pressure.

John Smith rolled up when the fun was over, and soon after 8.15

we had pressure up on *Firefly*, had coupled the Land-Rover on the back, and we were away. We took minor roads until we reached the A127, the Southend Arterial road, with the inevitable admiring glances from people on the pavements: remember, this was the Swinging Sixties, when the Beatles were all the rage and steam traction engines were almost as rare as snowstorms in August.

John and I were working as a team; I was kept busy with the injector and the shovel, little and often keeping *Firefly* going at a merry pace, while John looked after the steering. When we reached Basildon, a carnival official directed us to a private house where we topped up the water tanks while we topped up our own reserves with coffee and sandwiches.

Of course, we had a continuing stream of admiring onlookers, asking all manner of questions from the stupid to the well-informed, but one little boy was starting to annoy me with his repeated assertion that we had a leak. I told him that steam engines always leaked.

Soon we had taken our place in the procession around town and onto the carnival field. We were placed by the fairground amusements and belted up *Firefly* to power them, and to run our own canopy lights. That afternoon I could have gone back in memory to those fairgrounds of my childhood, with the puffing steam engine,

In the early days: 'Firefly' in the Hornchurch Carnival with the Land-Rover following. (Photo: Romford Recorder)

the roundabouts, and even the occasional sideshow. But reverie was brought to an end when a member of the carnival committee told us the wonderful news that we had won the first prize for vehicles: could we collect the cup at the 5pm presentations, in about half an hour?

That's probably when things started to go wrong. We packed up, ready to go, intending to collect the trophy on the way, but it was impossible to get near the central stage, even on foot. Somebody told us that the crowd was for a young man named Tony Blackburn from Radio Caroline, the pirate station aboard the *Mi Amigo* moored permanently off the Essex coast at Walton-on-the-Naze. And that was *before* he became famous!

We decided to collect the trophy later; we'd better get home before darkness fell. Soon we were steaming along the A127 at a steady pace, although the holiday traffic from Southend was quite heavy. And as we approached the notorious crossroads by the 'Halfway House' pub, we saw we were in a queue of traffic, not a happy position for a traction engine whose responses are nowhere near as keen as those of a small car.

I decided to put a little more water in the boiler; I turned on the water tap, then the steam cock, but *Firefly* did not pick up, and all I got was clouds of vapour.

"What's up?" John asked. "Injector up the creek?"

"Don't know. Try the one on the other side." John tried, but with the same result.

"God!" he groaned. "There's no water!"

I dipped a stick in the tank; it was dry, and there was a distinct trail of water along the road behind us. The safety valve was feathering and soon poor old *Firefly* would be blowing her top. We were in trouble — and stuck in a traffic queue!

"We've got to get over the cross-roads," John decided. "There's a lay-by we can use."

Feeling like a gambler in the last-chance saloon, I thrust the end of the lifter hose into the last of the water left in the last drum in the Land-Rover, and *Firefly* began sucking in her life-giving elixir. This quietened the now-blowing safety valve as I let as much water as I dared into the boiler, knowing *Firefly* could prime (get an air-lock) on the gradient at the crossroads.

Eventually we were over the crossing and we pulled onto the layby. John clambered under the tender, saw flaking paint which indicated the weak spot in the metal, and he was able to push his little finger through into the tank. With a hole that big it was impossible to move on, as we would lose all our water within minutes.

"I'll have to shove a bolt into it," John diagnosed from ground level. "Trouble is, Len, it's right up against the firebox; couldn't be in a worse place."

We found a spare bolt in the toolbox and managed to push it through the hole from the outside as the last of our water gurgled out. But there was still a sizeable gap around the bolt, and the risk that the bolt itself would rattle loose during the remainder of the journey home. And then I remembered the leaking oil drum of that morning: we still had the patch of sticky Sylglas. I peeled it off the drum, patted it home on the *out*side of *Firefly*'s tank, and the job was done. People tell me the pressure of water should have forced the seal off, but it did not.

However, we were waterless, except for what was in the boiler. Yet the Fates must have had some sympathy for us that day; the lay-by was the slip-road to a restaurant and a small service station — we still called them 'garages' in those days. Luckily the man on the forecourt recognised me as he was a customer at the Old Road Paint Works.

'Firefly' in the Romford Carnival. (Photo: Squire, Romford)

"There's only a little hose for topping up car rads — you can use that if you like, Len, but for God's sake keep your sparks away from the petrol pumps, or I'm out of a job."

It took us at least an hour to get a worthwhile quantity of water into the tank, but we dared not stay any longer as the sun was setting and *Firefly* had no headlights, sidelights, or traffic indicators — only her canopy lights.

Daylight was fading as I weighed up our predicament. If we kept on this dual carriageway we would find it next to impossible to cross from the slow lane to the fast lane and turn right, without lights. "I know a short cut over the Common," I told John. "It'll save a mile or so, but we need a bit of luck with oncoming cars."

A mile further on we filtered off the A127, and stopped on the bridge that took our minor road over that busy highway, to switch on the Land-Rover lights. They would, at least, provide rear lights and the headlamps would show the bulk of the steam engine. We would have to hope for the best at the front.

The last of the daylight faded as we still had that final mile to travel. Not only were we a hazard to any oncoming car, but I couldn't see the water gauge. I used the injector little and often, and I like to think we made it home in safety because I knew my engine — but it could have been down to pure luck.

THAT WAS THE last time I drove *Firefly* on the highway. I suppose it was a combination of several factors: the steam engine was getting too well known; I had had too many close calls with neighbours and inspectors; and I realised the risks involved in having a major breakdown on the road, even though caused through something as simple as a leaking tank.

It was *Firefly* who would have to go.

Little Lady could be garaged in *Firefly*'s shed, as she looked to the layman almost like an ordinary old lorry, not a steam engine. Also, the Foden would be easier to drive, and I had ideas about using her to tow the organ.

With some reluctance I put an advert in *World's Fair* — but I didn't bother with that clause about 'no time wasters'; it seemed a bit offensive.

It was a mistake. The first reply came as soon as the paper was published, and was from a man who claimed to have a commission to buy traction engines for export to conservationists; price, he said, would be no objection. He wanted to come the next day, and see the engine in steam.

I should have known. "Why not see the engine cold?" I asked. "It can often tell you more, and you can climb all over it."

"Sorry. I haven't the time. I have a roller and a road engine to see, and my customers want them quickly."

I gave in. "Come after six tomorrow and I'll steam her up." As I walked away from the phone I had my first misgivings; what potential customer would agree the price without seeing the goods? Only one who had no intention of buying. An uncle had warned me years ago: "Lad, if anyone tells you your asking price is alright — or even too low — start running, or he'll catch you out." I mentioned my doubts to Dee, my wife, and she suggested we go through the motions but be ready for tricks.

Firefly was polished as she was due to go to an exhibition, so at 5 o'clock I lit the fire. As soon as I had it going nicely, the phone rang. "It's the man who's coming at six," Dee hissed, handing me the receiver.

I took the phone. "Oh, Mr Brooks. Look — as you're going to steam up tonight, would you like me to come over and help? I could stoke it up, oil it, do any of those jobs."

Now I knew I had a timewaster. I hoped my voice didn't reflect my doubts when I told him six was the earliest time, as we ran a business from the premises. I'm sure you can appreciate the problems these timewasters cause: there are hours spent in firing, oiling, getting steam up, then after the demonstration the polishing, cleaning of the firebox and sweeping the fire tubes. There's also the cost of the coal, and half a day's pay for a man if you're not able to do it yourself.

I had just put the belt on the dynamo when my timewaster arrived. He looked younger than I had imagined and when he saw *Firefly* he gave himself away by dancing around the engine in excitement. He told me about the engine owners he knew, and described their engines, but he never asked any of the questions a prospective buyer would ask, nor did he mention his foreign customers.

Then I had to attend to the engine. I drained the cylinders, much to his delight. He was up on the footplate beside me as I started the flywheel turning, and was eagerly following everything I did.

I ran the dynamo up to 90 volts on the meter, but as I was about to put the injector on he put his hand on the regulator. "She's not up to a hundred volts yet."

I pulled his arm away, not bothering to hide my feelings. "Don't touch that — there are fifty bulbs on that circuit and the regulator's temperamental."

"What about the governors?"

"Not belted," I snapped. I managed to ease him off the footplate, then he wanted to know what she was like on the road. And still without a hint of wanting to buy.

I knew I was not going to drive around town on a fool's errand, and at that moment Dee called, as if by prearranged signal, which it was not: "You're wanted on the phone, Len. Long distance."

"Be there in a minute," I called back, urging the timewaster to the gate. "Sorry; no time for a road test. Give me a ring when you want to collect her."

He knew that I knew, but he was fighting a brave rearguard action. "I'll be in touch in a day or so."

It was nearly 8 o'clock before our timewaster made his departure, and I still had the clearing-up to do. "Genuine buyers only from now on!" I told Dee.

Several calls came in the next two days, and a few were steam-up requests. I told the callers that it was advisable to view an engine cold, and if they wanted to see it in steam they should come to our next carnival, but no way would they be allowed onto the footplate as we weren't insured for that risk.

That deterred the timewasters — but was I also turning away genuine buyers? Then a Wilfred Payne called from Yorkshire. He came down to Essex a few days later with his friend Mr Fearnley, a well-known engine owner in the north of England. They had a thorough inspection of *Firefly* — cold — and made me an acceptable offer. Within the week he had sent a low-loader down and *Firefly* was on her long journey up to Yorkshire.

It was a sad day for us all, seeing her go; dear old *Firefly* had given us many, many hours of pleasure, as well as a few scares. But, if this marked the end of one phase of my life, it also marked the beginning of the next — with *Ceōl*.

5: FAREWELL TO STEAM

WITH *FIREFLY* GONE, I turned my attention to *Little Lady*. I had already repaired her cab and, after a few minor jobs, she was ready for a road test.

Perhaps I should explain. The Ministry of Transport had recently introduced the compulsory road test of all motor vehicles on the tenth anniversary of their registration, which had sent thousands of pre-war rust-buckets to the scrap yards — although many were to be restored and reappear as classic cars in the years to come — but at that time there was no compulsory road test for steam-driven vehicles. And, as a matter of interest, the annual road tax for the Foden and her ilk was just £15.

But before that, I had a closer look at *Ceōl*, the 48-keyless organ (that means it can play 48 musical notes and it has no manual keyboard) built by Chiappa Ltd at some unrecorded date early in the century. The name is Irish and means 'music', and you pronounce the C as if it were a K — try Keeol. *Ceōl* was in *Firefly*'s old stable, and I opened the flaps in her side as far as the shed walls would allow. I plugged into the 240v domestic socket, and instantly the organ came to life; the lights came on, the blower filled the wind chest, and the music roller turned, but without a book to play. Obviously, when *Ceōl* had last been operated her owner had simply pulled the plug without switching off the individual components.

It was fascinating to see all these mechanical gadgets spring to life, and I grabbed the first book of music in the rack and thrust it into the keyframe. Immediately the shed was filled with the beautiful strains of *The Petite Waltz*.

I don't think I shall ever forget that tune, played under those conditions. I stepped down and gazed in admiration at the organ's rhythmical working, and its cadence as the final bars of the tune died away. Most of us have a few instances of pure magic in our lives, and that was one such moment for me.

I put another cardboard book into the frame, then another and another, forgetting that I may be annoying my neighbours even though I was enjoying every moment myself. I couldn't understand why I had waited so long to play *Ceōl*, and on that day a love affair was born between us — I like to feel that she responded — which was destined to endure for years and see us travel tens of thousands of miles together. I can truthfully say that *Ceōl* changed my life, as you will see.

But at this stage there were several regrets. I was receiving steady requests to take *Firefly* to fêtes and carnivals, and had to explain that she had gone, while *Little Lady* was not quite ready. Perhaps, I suggested as a compromise, you would like me to bring my fair organ *Ceōl*, towed by my Land-Rover? Almost all organisers agreed, and our first public appearance was scheduled for Brentwood.

There was much less preparation required; no steaming-up and very little polishing and, as *Ceōl* was now mounted in a close-coupled four-wheel trailer, I merely had to wipe off the dust that had gathered during storage, and we were ready.

I took my young nephew Maurice 'Mole' Newman — he was also nephew to my now-departed helper Les White — for this first performance in Brentwood; we were sited near the refreshment tent, with a power plug nearby, and we were soon playing to the crowds not only queueing at the tent but also drawn to listen to us in our own right. Mole quickly adapted himself to the keyframe, sorting out the music and — in later rallies — choosing the music to suit the mood. He learned how to adjust the speed of the frame to suit the melody, and the technical details such as tightening the base drum and adjusting the cymbals, which were also air-powered. It was so different, and so much easier, than manning a showman's traction engine. And when the day was over, how much easier it all was; just pack the music away, pull one flap down and another up and secure them with two locks — and we were ready for the road. But I still had a lump in my throat whenever I thought of *Firefly* far away in Yorkshire.

Yet there was still *Little Lady* to prepare for the road. Two weeks later I fired her up. Les was coming for the road test, and we planned to steam her up the A12 London-to-Great Yarmouth road, towards the capital for about five miles. Les was at the steering wheel with me attending to the fire, water, and regulator. We had a mere 300 yards to the A12, but the Foden seemed to lose steam at the sharp hump over the railway bridge. Once on the main road we opened her up a little, but after a mile or so she lost steam and we had to stop.

I wasn't happy about this, but after waiting around fifteen minutes we moved off, this time on low throttle. She kept steam better, but her speed was disappointing. We tried increasing the speed but were forced to take another rest, so we turned around and headed for home. The final ignominy was that we would have to wait for steam before we could climb that hump-bridge over the railway. Then I remembered the double-high for a short surge of power, and this ruse took us over the hump and back to the Old Road yard.

Disappointed with the road test, Les (who came back to help me on this) and I pulled the organ out of the shed and put the Foden in, before going our separate ways for a very late lunch. During my meal the phone rang. "Mr Brooks? I'm the lady living next to your factory. We think there's something wrong — we can hear water running."

"Don't panic; I'm on my way." I drove the two miles to Old Road but heard nothing more than the slight hiss of escaping steam and the crackle of cooling oil. There was a very low pressure reading on the gauge, but perhaps *Little Lady* made more noise than *Firefly*?

The worried neighbour was at her gate when I left. "I thought I'd better phone; you know we all get scared, thinking that that steam engine might explode."

I tried assuring her that nothing was wrong, but I knew the basic problem was that she was scared of *any* steam engine stored beside her house. That was one of the reasons why I had sold *Firefly* and, while I regretted the parting of the ways, I still wasn't happy with *Little Lady*. If she were going to bring me problems on the domestic front, as well as not performing properly . . . ?

I called a friend who knew Foden engines inside out; his advice was to experiment with the coal, probably mixing a little coke with it, and to check the blast.

The following weekend we forgot Fodens and their problems as Mole and I took the Land-Rover and *Ceōl* to a fête. We had no electrical pick-up point but as the truck had a power take-off which was coupled by two V-belts to an alternator between the cab seats, we had no problem.

We arrived early and parked the Land-Rover directly behind the organ. I was a little worried about using the truck's generator as the engine would have to run for several hours, giving a steady voltage without too much noise or fumes — and be economical. I needn't have worried. With the Land-Rover in top gear it merely ticked over and still drove the generator. The noise and fumes were negligible, and I never noticed the fuel gauge move. At four shillings a gallon — 20p in decimal money — the cost was not even noticed.

It was an easy day; there was virtually no supervision needed on the generator, and Mole was quite adept on the keyframe. I was ready for the next invitation, which came from John Arnott Brown, known to his friends as 'Newcastle' Brown, who was organising a steam rally at Denham, Bucks.

Although I was steamless I turned up, and enjoyed the rally; it was where I made new friends in Teddy Reed, Arthur Clarke and Bob Minny. The public really liked *Ceōl* and were intrigued by the Land-Rover's generator, but I was not yet aware how popular the organ was to become. Within days I was getting so many requests to appear at fêtes and other events that I had to start turning people away. In retrospect I realise that this was the beginning of the most hectic period of my life, and probably the most enjoyable as well, despite my nostalgia over *Firefly*.

It was Mole who took the invitation from the Brentwood Lions Club to bring *Ceōl* to a charity collection in the High Street. This was the organ's first venture into fundraising and, while I don't remember how much we raised that day, it was the beginning of a twenty-year bond with the town's Lions.

You must understand I didn't set out to raise money for charity, it was merely that *Ceōl* was the ideal instrument for the job and people were willing to give. Not long after, I was playing at a hospital fête and doing a bit of collecting, when I met Alan Pike. Now Alan worked for Dr Barnadro's Homes, as it was then called, as a fundraiser, and he could see *Ceōl*'s potential. He explained that the organ was an ideal centrepiece for a little show featuring clowns and other fancy costumes. Alan was so enthusiastic that I agreed to put in an appearance in the centre of Basildon and see what we could do.

It was a nice, sunny day: I was soon to learn that a good dose of sunshine could add 25% to any collection. And I was to learn that all Barnardo's projects were well-organised, which also helped. We started at 9.30 with a rousing march and soon had a crowd — probably half the people there had never seen a fairground organ since their childhood in prewar days, and the youngsters had never seen one at all.

The clowns clowned, the children were enthralled, the boxes jingled, and the pennies and tanners and bobs in those pre-decimal days, kept coming. At the end of the day our total was £140, a phenomenal sum when you consider that few people earned more than £20 in a week.

And then it was back to the problems with *Little Lady*. I must admit that *Ceōl*'s success had overshadowed anything I might do with the Foden, so I advertised her in *World's Fair*, using a box number to avoid the timewasters.

The replies came from all over the country. I could guess that a few were timewasters, and others would want to haggle over the price. One letter in particular criticised my so-called inflated asking price of £1,500 by quoting the cost from the builders, new, years earlier!

'Ceōl' and street collectors at Brentwood, Essex (Photo: Brentwood Gazette)

There were two letters which aroused particular interest. One was from George Cushing, who deserves special mention. George was born in the remote Norfolk village of Thursford and, like me, was spellbound by the bright lights of the fairground in the 1920s. As soon as he could afford to buy a steam engine, he did; then they began going out of favour as petrol engines took over. George kept buying while prices tumbled, and he was still buying when the market bottomed out and started to rise, as people realised that steam engines were now a novelty. George bought my *Little Lady* and put her in the barns on his Thursford farm, where he now held steam rallies, but as I write she is owned by the Bygone Heritage Village of Great Yarmouth.

Eventually, in 1977, George's motley assortment of steam engines and fairground memorabilia was to become the Thursford Collection, claimed to be the largest assembly of steam engines and similar treasures in the world. Among its exhibits is the theatre organ from the Tower Ballroom, Blackpool, that Reg Dixon — remember him? — played for 40 years. Thursford is now equally famous for its Christmas carol concerts which draw around 50,000 people a year.

George Cushing also saw *Ceōl* and asked me to give him a tune. I had to decline to avoid offending the neighbours — but if I had agreed, would George have made an offer for the organ as well? If so, my life would not have gone the way it did, and I would have been the loser.

Oh, I mentioned there were two letters of interest. The other was from an agent acting for collectors overseas, who asked me to phone him to arrange a steam-up trial. It was our old timewaster still at work.

6: WELCOME TO *CEŌL*

AFTER *LITTLE LADY* departed, I moved *Ceōl* into the big engine-shed and gave her a provisional facelift, mainly regilding the proscenium and improving the lighting. I had plans for a more major overhaul soon, now that I had become a dedicated organ owner.

For a start, *Ceōl* had to be installed in a smart motor vehicle. There were too many snags in the towing system: the trailer was heavy and difficult to manoeuvre, particularly in reverse; when I was playing the organ in a town centre, raising money for charity, I'd often find uncharitable policemen and traffic wardens who insisted the towing vehicle be removed to a car park — try *that* on a Saturday morning!

With the organ *inside* the van, I would be able to travel to one-day rallies easier and quicker, and nobody could ask me to put the van in the car park. And for two-day rallies, I could tow a caravan for overnight accommodation, and sleep on site.

I scanned the 'for sale' columns in the local press and in *World's Fair* until I found a year-old Ford Transit that had been used as a demonstration vehicle for a firm that sold washing machines and the like. It was wired with plenty of 240v power points, it had a 4kw generator aboard, and it was in good order. Furthermore, it was the first ad I replied to, and I was the first person to reply to this ad.

She was mine for £500, probably not a bargain at the time but, looking back at it over the years, it must have been the bargain of my life. I travelled more than 120,000 miles in that van and as I write it's still going perfectly strong and will probably hit 200,000 miles.

Now for the modification, which took only a few days. A local coach builder cut away the nearside (passenger's side) panel and fitted *Ceōl* inside so that when we were parked by the pavement,

'Ceōl' and the Transit van take corner position at a small event.

she looked out at the passing pedestrians. We replaced the van's side panel as two flaps, the top one hinged at the top and held open by two twisted-brass rods, like those supporting *Firefly*'s canopy. The bottom flap was hinged at the bottom and, when open, rested on the ground. On the inside thus revealed I painted a landscape of a lake and mountains.

I gave plenty of attention to the lighting. After all, organs are a part of show-business and need attractive lights. I put a row of 50-watt bulbs along the top flap, surrounded the hole in the van's side with more, not being too economical with them, and then added four at 25-watts each to light the glockenspiel, the 'bell-play'. There were more lights behind the drums at the back of the organ.

You're still with me? I then turned my attention to the proscenium, the very front of the stage. When I bought *Ceōl* she ran on 110v DC, understandable as she was built for fairground use. The wind was supplied by a powerful DC blower, and the keyframe was driven by a compact little universal electric motor coupled by a flexible drive to a gearbox. The gearbox reduced the speed to the V-pulley, and it was the wheel at the other end of that V-belt which drove the keyframe. You're *still* with me?

54

I was grateful that the motor had two voltage settings — 110DC and 230 AC — as that was soon to prove useful. Finally, I inserted a large adjustable resistance in series with the electricity supply to the keyframe drive motor, and so gave the operator a wide range of playing speeds. Now, as almost all mains electricity is on 230v AC, when I wanted to use the organ from the town supply, I merely had to make a quick change — hence the big transformer and metal rectifier which converted the 230v AC into 110v DC.

I suppose I could have changed the whole system to AC only, as used by the new age organ builders, but because I'm something of a traditionalist I decided to keep to the DC basics. As it happened I'm glad I did, because I often coupled to traction engines when visiting steam rallies — and they're all 110v DC.

You *are* still with me?

My modifications meant that all the wiring and all the 13-amp plugs already in the Transit, became 110v DC once I had wired in the transformer and rectifier. So I fed the incoming 230v AC through a switchboard and ammeter to show the total load. I also wired the 110vDC circuit through a DC ammeter on a switchboard, which became useful when I needed to reduce the load.

There was a minor complication. The entire lighting system had to run on either 240v or 110v bulbs, so I chose the latter. This was no problem at the outset but it presented increasing difficulties as time went by, because 110v bulbs were being phased out.

And to complete the electrical arrangement, I fitted a double-pole, double-throw switch, the AC side connecting the transformers to a flexible lead, with the ordinary 3-pin plug to pick up the 230v AC supply. The 110v lead was connected direct to the DC side, cutting out the transformer and rectifier, and on the other end of it was a cable that would be used to link up with the dynamo on a show-man's engine. When not in use this cable was coiled up and stowed away.

The back of the Transit was quite spacious. There was ample room in the Luton top (the space over the cab) for tools, brooms, oilskins and miscellaneous items; the opening was panelled on each side and I fitted a curtain across. To the right went the switchboard — the two ammeters, a DC and an AC voltmeter, and a pair of terminals that I could connect up to recharge the Transit's battery. Below the Luton top, two wide shelves served as storage for the musical books.

'Ceōl' on tour.

There were no big jobs to do on the interior of the vehicle as it was neatly panelled and very tidy. The organ fitted snugly, and there was only a little carpentry needed. The rear doors were double-sectioned, which was just right for display — people like to see how things work, and these doors opened the full width of the van.

When the modification was done, *Ceōl* looked and sounded very professional. She was soon to begin a new phase in her life — and so was I.

IT'S STRANGE HOW history repeats itself — or is it that seafaring runs in certain families? As Maurice, my nephew Mole, was helping at a Sunday garden party at Hornchurch Council offices, he told me that I would be losing his services as keyframe helper. You remember that his uncled Les bought a boat and sailed away into the proverbial sunset? Now young Mole announced that he had joined the Merchant Navy. The party had been a great success as it had attracted a scattering of stars from stage and television — but none of them would replace Mole.

Sensing my disappointment, Mole volunteered his mother's services — I later learned that it was with her knowledge — so I gained two worthy assistants to replace the one I had lost. Two? Oh, yes

— Mole's mother Irene would bring her sister Doris along. You should have guessed it: as Mole was my nephew, his mother's sister Doris, better known as Dee, was my wife!

Very soon Irene, Dee and I fell into the weekend routine of doing the rounds of steam rallies, fêtes, carnivals, open days, special days, charity events, and anything else that came our way.

It was much easier with a husband and wife team, and no great problem when sister-in-law came along as well. We had no pets and our daughters were able to look after themselves, so on most Friday or Saturday mornings we shut up the house, collected Irene, and drove off to the event.

If we were performing at some stately home, or just in an open field in the country, we'd drop the caravan where everybody else was unhitching theirs, and set up shop. We'd have coffee and sandwiches in the Transit so we could each have a break, and we could take it in turns to wander around and see what other people were doing: there's no point in going to a rally if you don't see anything but your own vehicle!

Sometimes the lavatories were a problem, as at Holton in Oxfordshire where in the early days the toilet pan was in a simple shed and the urinal was a folded corrugated iron trough. I remember an older boy saying to his smaller brother: "No good you coming in here; you'd cut yourself badly."

And when the day was over we'd go back to the Elddis caravan for dinner. Both women are good cooks, and usually managed to give us a decent meal with the aid of a fridge and oven powered by bottled propane gas, with the emphasis on salads, bacon and eggs, and chops with veg. The sleeping arrangements were with two single bunks in each of two rooms, split by a dividing curtain.

The charity collecting was coming along nicely, too. Alan Pike, who'd introduced himself to me at Brentwood, had been back and together we had planned a series of collections in the main towns in my part of the country — see the appendix for the list.

My ambition then was to top two hundred pounds for Dr Barnado's, which would take some doing in pennies and ha'pennies — there were 240 ha'penny coins to the pound — and I well remember how we hit that first target. The collectors were bringing in their boxes and Ceōl was playing The Last Waltz, my closing-down tune, when a man gave us a five-pound note: real money in those days.

He explained that he was a Barnado's old boy and was repaying some of his debt now that he was successful in business.

With the two hundred pound target thus reached, we set ourselves higher levels, just at the time that other charities approached us to help them. Now, I'm an easy-going chap and I don't mind helping where I can, but soon the requests were coming in so fast that I had to have our private telephone number changed, and go ex-directory. I told my regular contacts of the new number, and it didn't affect the phone at the paint works which was on a different number. In any event, now I had sold *Firefly,* we weren't advertising the Old Road business.

I suppose we might have lost a few bookings with the organ as well, but we were still kept busy. I loved *Ceōl*, and I thoroughly enjoyed our new life-style but I must confess I still missed *Firefly*, whenever I had time to be nostalgic. The irony of it was that those complaining neighbours moved within a month of my selling *Little Lady* and the new owners were sympathetic towards steam engines and fair organs. Isn't that just the way it goes?

It was on a sizzling weekend in June when we were at a two-day flower show in Northampton that *Ceōl* failed us for almost the only time in our travels. She lost volume. There was no change in pitch or tempo as when a manual gramophone is running down; it was as if she were a portable radio with flat batteries. We soon diagnosed the trouble: the blower was too hot, and the overheated air just would not give the volume. I tried putting a dampened sponge by the air intake, but it didn't work, and there was nothing else I could think of. I was really humiliated at having taken my organ to the party but not being able to play.

And so, when we got home, I had to turn for help to Victor Chiappa. I had met Victor many times at the shows but as I had yet to visit his factory in the heart of London, I was pleased when he invited me to call one Sunday morning, the only day of the week when parking restrictions were lifted.

Of course, it wasn't a scorcher of a day when I parked the Transit and *Ceōl* in Eyre Street, EC1. He listened attentively when I played the machine, and he made a few adjustments. "Your problem sounds as if it was blower failure, Len. It's moderately common on really hot days."

"So what do we do?"

"The only real option is to fit a bellows, but even that could fail at times. In any case, you can't fit it directly to the organ."

Victor told me he could make a set of bellows that would stand behind the keyframe, which meant that air would have to be fed in to the wind chest, an air reservoir, through a three-inch trunk pipe. There was, he pointed out, plenty of room behind the organ. "Now let's have a poke around downstairs."

Going down into the Chiappa basement in the middle of London in the late 1960s was like stepping back in time; I felt as if I had returned to some sweatshop in Dickensian days, where parts of organs from the late nineteenth century were scattered among belt-driven machinery made of heavy steel castings. It was chaos — but, dare I say it, orderly chaos.

Victor waved at a table-like object in a far corner. Clearing miscellaneous pieces of wood from it he exposed a fairly sturdy pair of bellows fitted under the tabletop. As he pulled the gadget clear he mused: "Good God! We've had this thing more years than I care to remember! We used it for air-testing organs until somebody invented a blower."

I measured the bellows and decided it would fit in the van, and Victor judged he could rebuild it quickly. "That'll give you all the air you need, no matter how hot it is."

"Okay — I'll have it. How long?"

He rubbed his chin. "Couple of weeks should do it."

Two Sundays later I drove Ceōl back to Eyre Street and was amazed at the transformation Victor had made in that dusty set of bellows. He had completely re-leathered it, and had fitted a new counter-shaft and bearings to drive the main crankshaft, which now actuated two feeders which in turn pumped the bellows. The final drive came via a stepped-cone V-belt from the electric motor, giving scope to vary the speed. And the beauty of it was that the device would be simple and easy to adjust on site; but the thing was beautiful in its own right, nicely painted and polished, not looking too modern, and fitting the gap between the back of the organ and the far side of the van, leaving adequate space to stand and operate the keyframe.

"That looks just wonderful, Victor!"

"Right. Let's give it a try."

We rough-mounted the bellows in the van and I saw how simple it was to slip the existing blower away and connect the flexible trunk pipe from the new bellows straight into the wind chest. Victor had put in a ⅓hp 230v AC motor for the test, so we had to run a special lead from this as all the power plugs in the organ were 110v DC. This was no problem and soon the new bellows was pumping merrily, the music was playing, and the wind chest exhausting, so we were able to cut down the drive speed a little.

"Try not to race the bellows, Len," Victor advised.

"Fine; I'll remember." I gloried in the sight of all these moving parts and I knew that, with the Transit's rear doors open, spectators would have a perfect view of the working mechanism.

Back home, I fixed the bellows securely and installed a 110v DC motor drive which I had bought from an Army-surplus store for just £3. That was a wonderful motor; it could start under full load, and as I write it has given more than twenty years' service without failing.

Oh — and I picked up some extra music books from Victor's workshop.

THE NEXT RALLY was in Hertfordshire and, as I suspected, the bellows interested the crowds. It also interested the owner of another organ who made some facetious remarks. I just put it down to jealousy.

7: RETURN TO STEAM

DEE AND I were at a weekend steam rally at Weeting, near Brandon in Suffolk — the village has the ruins of a castle well worth exploring — when I met *Prince*, and decided to go back into the steam engine business.

By now we had settled into a routine, the Transit towing the caravan and so allowing us to spend almost every weekend at a rally; back in the sixties organisers definitely preferred exhibitors who would stay for both the Saturday and Sunday.

It was early on the Sunday morning, long before the public arrived, that I was strolling across the meadow and saw a beautiful miniature steam traction engine gently puffing towards me. As it came closer I recognised my good friend Walter Rasberry at the controls.

"Hello, Walter. My word, that's a lovely engine; how did you come by her?"

Walter stopped, and stepped out of the tender — I couldn't say he stepped *down* because he stood taller than the top of the engine's smokestack.

"Come by it, boy? I *built* her," he said proudly. He shovelled some coal into the fire. "Built her from a set of castings made by a local firm. I had the boiler made by professional manufacturers, but the rest I did myself in the workshop. Not bad, is she?"

I had to admire the machine, perfect in every detail and built at a scale of 4.5 inches to the foot, or 9:24. A brass plaque on her smoke box read 'Charles Burrell & Sons Limited, Thetford, England', the only thing about her that was not genuine, as she had never seen the inside of Burrell's factory.

"Of course, she really needs a proper paint job, and lining to Burrell standards," Walter added.

I sighed in envy, memories of *Firefly* coming back to haunt me. "My God, Walter," I breathed. "I'd love an engine like this. She's more than a model; she's a proper working traction engine."

"Aye. She weighs more'n half a ton, and I get her up to a hundred and ten pounds pressure." Walter sat nonchalantly on the rim of the tender.

"How about making me one?" I couldn't resist it. "You don't know how much I'd love to own an engine just like this. She's a beauty!"

Walter teased me. "I'll think it over, Len."

I watched in envy as he steamed away, and I couldn't forget him and his little engine all day. It joined the full-size engines in the afternoon's grand parade and drew more than its share of applause. If ever a man longed for an unattainable beauty, that was me that Sunday afternoon. Finally I went over to Walter's pitch and dropped another hint about his making a duplicate for me. "Tell you what," I said, more in jest than in expectation, "you let me have this one, and you can build yourself another."

As Walter seemed to be considering my suggestion, time appeared to stand still. Finally he nodded. "Alright, Len. We have ourselves a deal if the money's right."

You know how people say they were walking on air? That's how I felt as I hurried back to Dee to tell her the news. But I was worried at the same time; worried that Walter would go back on his word. I was worried all the way home, and all the way out to Walter's place at Grimston, near King's Lynn where, you remember, he ran the petrol station and motor repair workshop.

Walter never changed his mind, but I could see he was reluctant to part with the model Burrell. We had a few glasses of Walter's home-made wine to help him drown his sorrows.

The little traction engine had no name at this stage, but soon my daughters chose the apt title of *Prince*, ideal for a junior version of a king of the road. Although it was a masculine name, I couldn't help thinking of 'him' as *her*, she was so dainty, so beautiful, and looking so fragile compared with a full-size engine. But at half a ton, there was nothing much feminine about her!

I had plans for *Prince*. I didn't buy her to puff around in; she wasn't a toy. She was a powerful steam engine with a cylinder bore of 3.25 inches and a stroke of 3.75in, and she was going to provide the power for *Ceōl*, if I had my way.

Here was my plan — but would it work? I took a broad, flat pulley, 4in in diameter, and fitted it to the end of the counter shaft on the

Clowns help 'Ceol' collect for Barnardo's in Basildon (Photo: Southend Evening Echo)

bellows. All I needed now was a length of flat belting to couple to the engine's flywheel, and — *hey, presto!* — I had a real steam-driven organ to take to the rallies. It was so simple in theory: now it was time to put it to the test.

I parked the Transit van in the shed with its rear doors open; I pushed *Prince* in behind *Ceōl* and lined up the belt from the steam engine's flywheel to *Ceōl*'s pulley wheel. Then I took off the belt and closed the van's rear doors; you'll see why in a moment.

I had devised a way of getting *Prince*'s steam up quicker than usual, by putting a heater fan from an old car into the top of her chimney and wiring it to the Land-Rover's battery. I then lit the kindling wood in the normal way, switched on the fan, and the induced air current had the fire burning well in around fifteen minutes — but the smoke was too dense for comfort, which is why I'd closed the Transit's rear doors.

Only those people fortunate enough to have managed a steam engine will know the exhilarating experience of raising steam; on this day the excitement was even greater because the experience was both explorative and experimental.

As soon as I had a fair head of steam I opened the drain cocks and had the motion idling, which brought the fire along nicely and soon reached working pressure, with the safety valve lifting at exactly 115psi. I tested the water feed pump and found it satisfactory.

Now for the steam drive. I opened the van's rear doors, slipped the belt in place, and very carefully opened *Prince*'s regulator. Would the idea work? Was the engine powerful enough? Those last doubts flashed through my mind in the seconds it took to fill the bellows. *Prince*'s engine was only just idling, proof that she had sufficient power but, as the load increased the draught on the fire, I put the damper almost shut.

Of course, I just *had* to try a tune! The first problem was that my hands were oily, as you would expect. I climbed up onto *Ceōl* and found the second problem: the smoke was irritating. Ignoring that for the moment I gingerly put a tune into the keyframe with my fingertips and there, in all her glory, *Ceōl* was playing — and driven by steam power.

The next stage was to get the combination mobile. As I knew a good trailer maker I soon had what I wanted: a two-wheeler with four stout corner legs, and a coupling which would fit both the Land-

Rover and the Transit van. The idea was that at rallies the traction engine would stand permanently in its trailer, so avoiding the problems of loading off and on, and having to park the trailer. I also ordered an extension to *Prince*'s chimney to take the smoke clear of *Ceōl*, and while these two jobs were in progress I painted the engine and had it lined, the resulting combination of traditional red and green looking extremely smart. The final touch was a brass plate with *Prince*'s name embossed on it.

With everything in place, I had another experimental steam-up, but this time it was painfully slow to build up pressure, probably because of the resistance offered by the extended chimney. I didn't want to use the 12-volt heater fan because, although it worked, I knew there had to be a better way. It was a problem I would have to keep at the back of my mind and answer some other day. But the taller chimney meant there was no smoke in *Ceōl* and *Prince*'s engine steamed magnificently. I made this trial an extended, non-stop run, and when I couldn't fault the set-up in any way, I decided we were ready for a public performance.

I contacted the organiser of the Medway Rally, whom I knew as Roddy, and told him what I could offer. He was favourably impressed and invited us to the event, scheduled to be held at Chatham in May.

We knew we would have to plan this outing very carefully: it would be too embarrassing if anything were to go wrong. We decided that I would drive the Transit with *Ceōl*, towing *Prince* on her trailer, while Dee would haul the caravan with the Land-Rover. Long before the day we had drawn up lists of everything we thought we might need, down to the tube brush for *Prince*'s boiler. *Prince*, of course, was solidly blocked on her trailer to prevent the slightest movement, and she was then securely roped to rings on the trailer. Finally, on the last night before the rally we sheeted the engine under its own tailor-made tarpaulin. We were confident we had everything under control, as well as under cover.

The journey, through the Dartford Tunnel, was uneventful, but setting up at Chatham gave us some problems as we were pitched out on a field, not on a hard surface such as the concrete yard back home. It took a great deal of time and patience to set the flat belt to the pulley and, although the day was still young, the engine was attracting plenty of attention by the time I had got up steam, and the inquisitive spectators made moving around quite difficult.

Almost a museum in its own right; the Lampit workshop at Banbury. (Photos: Jim Edwards)

We played to a sizeable crowd on both days, but I found one big snag that wasn't apparent in our yard tests. Sunday was quite breezy and on occasions the belt blew off, much to the consternation of tape recordists. But on reflection, the launch of the steam drive was a great success, and the icing on the cake was a featured report and pictures of *Prince* and *Ceōl* in Friday's copy of *World's Fair*.

I had to go back to the workshop to cure that belt problem, which could be much worse during really inclement weather. I decided to fit a dynamo bracket on *Prince*'s smoke box, and to that I bolted a counter shaft, on one side of it a wide flat pulley and on the other side a V-pulley; in future the drive to operate the bellows would be a long V-belt to a three-step cone pulley.

This not only stopped the problem of the belt being blown off, it also added flexibility inasmuch as we could belt up to the organ with no meticulous lining-up problem, and we could also adapt the engine to work at its best speed by moving the belt onto the various steps of the cone pulley. The only flat belt was a short one linking the flywheel to the counter shaft.

The yard test was enlightening. I was able to increase the engine speed and so lower the bark of the exhaust and make the general performance better.

It was during this steam-up that I slipped the flexible hose from

Perhaps a little too loud, here at the Suffolk Show?

the snare drum, which allowed the air from the bellows to excape in a nice gentle draught, and I wondered why I hadn't thought of it earlier. All I needed now was a length of flexible hose, a hole cut in the extension chimney, and a metal elbow pipe to deflect the air up the flue. I rigged up the new idea then started the firing-up by using the electric motor to drive the bellows which sent the air up the chimney. It worked perfectly: the firing was easy and, better still, *Ceōl* was always free of smoke. And so *that* problem was cured.

The publicity from a *World's Fair* write-up on my combination brought instant response, and I was invited to rallies all over the country. You must remember that in the sixties there were far less rallies than there are today, but *Prince* had given me the *entré* to most of them, as I had something unusual, if not unique.

But would I start a trend?

I was soon to have the answer for, after only three weeks, I was surprised to see at a show somebody's attempt to jump on my metaphoric bandwagon by belting up a freelance traction engine to a small organ. I was interested — and, I suppose, a little gratified — to see he had the same problems that I had. The smoke was unbearable, but I didn't see the belt come off because the engine could not steam well enough to keep the organ playing for more than a few minutes. Not surprisingly, it was the only time I saw this attempt.

As for us, *Ceōl* and *Prince* were getting great write-ups in the provincial press, and nice pictures in *Model Engineer*.

I basked in the sunshine of those reports and the resultant phone calls and invitations after the Medway rally. You must remember that until the early seventies there were no 4.5in Burrell miniature engines at all at rallies, and the advent of what I call the 'neo-organ' was still some years away. In those times I came across only one organ that was built by its owner, and he was Peter Bish. By the way, the last time I saw Peter's handiwork it was still in excellent voice.

In years to come, promoters wouldn't want too many organs as they caused a cacophony when they were sited too closely — but that was a problem strictly for the future. And now that I had something to keep me busy, I decided to make a big change in my future: I was going to retire from making paint.

8: INTO ACTIVE RETIREMENT

I HAD LONG decided to retire fairly young, and in 1972, at the age of 62, I sold the paint business. It was too small to be of interest to the big boys but I had an offer from a firm in Northamptonshire which was interested in making emulsion paint, then rapidly gaining in popularity. Production went up to Bradford but the retail side of the business stayed in Harold Wood and is still going strong today as Leonard Brooks's Successors. The pebble mill has gone, and a row of houses now stands on the site; I have dreams of the owners being awakened in the small hours by the ghostly rumble of that mill!

Some people said I sold up because of the preservation bug, but truthfully it was not. Yet I must admit I don't know what I would have done to occupy myself if I hadn't been travelling the country with *Ceōl*.

My first rally in retirement was at Walpole St Andrew, a lovely little village near King's Lynn, Norfolk. It was April, and I still remember the cold wind that blew in straight from The Wash five miles away. A fellow exhibitor told me: "You know the trouble? There's only one telegraph pole between us and the North Sea!" I learned later that the locals have another name for the North wind: a lazy wind. "That doon't goo round you," they say, "that goo stret through!" And, in truth, there was nothing — apart from that telegraph pole — between us and the North Pole. Or Siberia, if you cared to keep on going.

After Walpole, I kept a diary of my travels and charity collections — see the appendix — which has given me great pleasure over the years, both for reference and for the memories that the records bring back. It's not totally accurate and you may find a few gaps.

I must tell you about the charity collections. After raising that first £200 it was natural we should want to increase our target. The real break came with the change to decimal currency — Mickey Mouse money, as we called it — in 1971. It was as if people temporarily lost a feeling for the value of cash, as if they were on holiday and spending foreign currency. The attitude certainly made *Ceōl*'s totals leap, and in the first collection with the new 'pees', and with some of the old stuff thrown in, we made a comfortable £364!

After this, the totals went from strength to strength. I remember Alan Pike saying to me on one occasion: "They're putting in lots of two-bobs today, just as they would have put in tuppence last year." (If you've forgotten, the two bob was today's 10p, and tuppence (2d) was around 1p.) But the total that day was £470.

Some while later, *Ceōl* did a big Christmas charity collection in Romford Market for the old people of the town, and we raised more than £600: was there no end to it? I remember Romford was a great pitch, but certain stallholders complained about the music; a friendly policeman suggested that it upset them seeing money going into the collection tins. They had the last word, as music was banned in the market after that.

The next rally after Walpole was at Grays, Essex. My memories of that event are not so good. We didn't take *Prince* so I plugged *Ceōl* into an electric socket in a council-owned building. The staff knocked off promptly at 5.30 and locked the door with my cable trapped, leaving me no alternative but to cut the live cable. Luckily I had a pair of insulated pliers with me, but I'm glad to report I heard the fuse explode.

We moved on to the Great Missenden Steam Rally in Buckinghamshire, a really nice show in beautiful surroundings. Teddy Read, an organ owner from the Amersham area, was there with his Gavioli 89-key organ and I recall him saying to me: "Len, you've got the only steam-driven organ, but watch out: there'll be people copying." I didn't take *Prince* to the next event, the two-day Dagenham Town Show, as I had doubts about the engine's safety: the kids sometimes got a little high-spirited in that part of the world.

And then came the three-day Knebworth Rally held in the grounds of the stately home. We arrived early and took part in drumming up support and interest by playing in most of the villages between Stevenage and Welwyn Garden City with the owner, Lord David Cobbold of the East Anglian brewing family, joining us for the fun.

Knebworth House itself is a wonderful place; it was begun in 1492 and was mostly rebuilt in 1843 by Sir Edward Bulwer-Lytton, who

70

wrote *The Last Days of Pompeii*, and both Dickens and Disraeli have stayed there. But our interest was in the big steam rally and fair in the vast grounds. My friends George and Sylvia were there with their enormus caravan and Robey traction engine. I never knew their surnames; George is now dead and Sylvia married a Mr Dudley.

It's not so far from Knebworth to Milton Keynes, if you're just counting miles, but if you're counting years then there's close on five centuries. From the great Tudor mansion we went to the New City Show to promote a satellite community that wasn't even built: I knew the area as Bletchley, the nearest existing town.

That's where I met Tod Cody, one of the greatest showmen I was ever to know. Tod was renowned for doing his job to perfection and I recall the main event he had staged for that show. It was based on one of Houdini's tricks: a man was strapped into a straightjacket, bound in chains, then hauled by his ankles to hang upside down at the end of a rope suspended from the jib of a gigantic crane, reaching maybe two hundred feet high. And then they set fire to the rope.

It was exciting stuff, but there was the inevitable know-it-all who told me: "It's not what it seems, you know. There's a wire cable through the middle of that rope."

Leonard with 'Ceōl.'

I assumed everybody watching must know that, but it didn't detract from the thrill of hoping the man would escape in time. "So what do you want for your five bob?" I asked the know-all. "Blood?"

Prophetic words? Several years later Tod Cody tried the stunt himself and fell. He was seriously injured and lucky to escape death, but he eventually recovered.

The New City Show was a success, of course, and led to *Ceōl* attending several of Tod's promotions in Milton Keynes, the last one being in the mammoth shopping centre; it was something of a shock seeing a town spring up in so short a time.

We were well into the rally circuit by now. Northampton, followed by the big Knowl Hill event and always one of my favourites. Then the Bysteam Rally on the outskirts of Norwich, back to Chelmsford, then up to Roxton Park near Bedford for another well-organised event.

Retired? At times it felt as if I were back in a full-time job, except that it was thoroughly enjoyable, my life's ambition coming true. And in case you're wondering about the finances let me say that all we got for attending these events was expenses. Sometimes they were a bit tight, sometimes a bit generous, but there was no way anybody could make a living out of going the rounds of steam shows.

Soon we were into September and, I thought, the end of the rally engagements for the year. But I was wrong. After a few local organ-only outings we were invited to a steam rally at Paddock Wood near Tonbridge, in the heart of the Kentish Weald.

And it was here that I met the fair organ *Simulator*. I call it an organ, yet it was really an artifice with an organ-like front but without the proper workings; it played fairground organ tunes from a tape recorder. I feel you must have a strong stomach to take a device like that to a rally, but the joke among us *real* organ owners was that there were actually tape recordists taping the music!

And still the season hadn't ended! In mid-October we were at Hadlow Down, near Crowborough in Sussex, for one of the longest-established rallies. And then we were invited to Kemsley Mill near Sittingbourne, Kent, for the closing meet of the Sittingbourne Light Railway, a line which originally took finished newsprint from the papermill to the main line, from where it went to Kemsley Newspapers.

When we got home from Sittingbourne I was planning to drain

the water from *Prince*'s boiler and lay her up for the winter, but in the post was an invitation to attend a steam fair and firework show in Fulford Barracks, York, organised by Doubtfires Amusements, a company well-known in the North of England.

The North Country? This would be new territory for us with *Prince* and *Ceōl*, and it would be in mid-November. But, as the weather looked to be holding, we decided to go. We left home early on the Thursday, with Dee and her sister Irene sharing the driving of the Land-Rover and towing the caravan, while I towed *Prince* on her trailer behind the Transit van carrying *Ceōl*. We arrived in York just as the light was fading, so giving us most of the next day to settle in before the show started on Friday evening.

All through Friday the traction engines and fair organs and other exhibitors came in, and I found myself a minor celebrity as engine and organ owners from the North Country greeted us, many of them expressing an interest in *Prince*, having seen reports and pictures of her in *World's Fair* and modelling magazines. That day I learned that there were quite a number of model engineers who were working on engines like mine.

When I met Enoch Doubtfire, the man behind the weekend's extravaganza, he expresed his particular thanks that we had travelled so far to come to his show. It was, he explained again, not the usual rally-type event since the engines, a number of which were showman's type locomotives, were there to demonstrate as near as possible the kind of work for which they were built, be it generating electricity or providing mechanical power for threshing machines and steam ploughs.

Friday evening was a fantasy come to life, with the smell and sound of traction engines gently puffing away, and the glitter of lights around their canopies and on the other sideshows; it was almost like the fairgrounds of my childhood.

Saturday was another day of pure nostalgia, but when darkness fell there was the greatest firework display I have ever seen, with rockets and cascades and shellbursts in a wonderland of colours — and all this on top of the thrill of another evening of fairground magic. I was living my boyhood dreams, although only a few months had passed since I began my retirement.

When we were at York I was surprised to meet Sylvia and George, our friends from Aspley Guise in Buckinghamshire, minus their engine, as they had come up just to see the show. When I casually mentioned that this was one of the best ways I could imagine to end the rally season, George had a surprise for me.

"End of the season, Len? Oh, no! We want you to come to our giant bonfire night next week!" To whet my appetite they told me about the huge bonfires that they always had an their event.

Their Firework Night was in a typical old-world setting in the heart of beautiful countryside not so far from Milton Keynes. The local ladies had baked lots of goodies; George had his Robey showman's type engine under steam with full capony lights glowing, and he also wired lights to the stalls and provided electric power for *Ceōl*; I didn't take *Prince* on this trip.

You'll forgive an old man his reminiscences, I hope, but that bonfire was the biggest I have ever set eyes upon. It was built on a base of old railway sleepers, which had had years of tar and creosote doses soaked into them, and it made a pillar of fire so big it looked as though we had our own volcano on hand. They told me the pile smouldered for days afterwards.

But we still hadn't finished for the season! After the excitement of the rallies and the other engagements, in the last week of November we started a short season of town-based charity collections. We began in Watford and worked our way through Romford, Hornchurch, Billericay, Harold Wood and Brentford.

When finally we packed up for my first Christmas in retirement, I had a little time to look back on a truly remarkable year, and a busy and exciting one as well, and I had to admit that I was undeniably hooked on organs and engines. In that season, beginning in April, we had visited thirty locations and had played *Ceōl* on fifty-one days. We must have had beginners' luck, because we'd had no serious problems. I knew that situation could not last — and my diary for the next year, 1974, was already well booked up.

Life looked interesting — very interesting.

9: ON THE RALLY CIRCUIT

I SPENT THE winter touching up the paintwork and doing minor repairs, and usually had a book of tunes going through the organ as I worked; as Victor Chiappa said — organs were like human beings, and had to breathe properly to sing.

Ceōl's first outing was in Romford Market on 10 March, for the British Legion, and I made it an organ-only event as I didn't consider it practical to take a steam engine into town centres. The first show for both *Ceōl* and *Prince* was a fête on 14 April, held in the spacious grounds of the National Children's Home at Harpenden, Herts, and it was here that I first saw *Prince*'s rival — a 4.5in-scale Burrell traction engine, almost identical to *Prince* except that its rear wheels were much narrower. For the first time I appreciated what Walter Rasberry had told me: wider wheels not only gave greater traction but also enhanced the engine's appearance.

The owner of this engine asked how long it had taken me to build *Prince*, and when I confessed that I hadn't built her I felt just a little ashamed, as if I had cheated.

He answered, totally without rancour: "I don't know how anyone could part with an engine like that, after spending so many hours building it." We chatted for a while, then he puffed away on his engine to join the other model engineers with their steam railway. Our meeting gave me food for thought: a person's interests are either in building an engine such as *Prince*, or in running it — seldom do you find somebody interested in both aspects of the modelling craze. Think of those hours spent at rallies, when you could be at home in the workshop. But if you're a builder, it's a shame to let your finished work stand idle — so what does one do? Maybe Walter had the right idea all along? *Prince*, meanwhile, went on plying the organ with wind.

From the National Children's Home we went into Watford for a collection for the local Lions in aid of handicapped children, and raised several hundred pounds.

The next big event was a two-day Whitsun steam show at Bulmer's Railway Centre in Hereford, the retirement home of the famous Great Western Railway locomotive *King George V*, the first of the 4-6-0 'King' class locomotives. Built in 1927 and last used in 1967, it was restored at Bulmer's works and hauled the company's six-coach Pullman Cider Train on special occasions such as this. As I remember, I was fortunate enough to meet Vernon Miles, the locomotive's driver, who found as much fascination in diminutive *Prince* as I did in his enormous engine.

The contrasts between the giant and the dwarf were never more apparent than when I told him that five hundredweight (250kg) of coal would give me three days of continuous driving, and he replied: "I put that much in each corner of the firebox, just to get the fire going!" I was in my element when Vernon invited me to come up on the footplate when he put *King George V* back in her shed.

The show went well until Whit Monday, when rain started in the morning. It didn't deter the crowds, but it certainly made conditions underfoot more difficult. I had been talking steam with a certain reverend Mr Miles, who was well-known in steam preservation and who owned a big Fowler showman's engine, when I said in a moment of pique: "Could you ask the grand architect of the universe to ease the rain for today?" Several hours later, as a watery sun began peeping through the clouds, he came back to me. Holding his hands as if prayer, he said: "Best I could do."

The rain slowly cleared and I managed to forget the weather altogether as I watched Vernon Miles and his helpers put *King George V* to bed at the end of two busy days of steam. What a contrast between that king among kings, and my tiny *Prince*!

Home on Tuesday, then on Friday we went to Wandle Park at Merton, in south-east London, followed by my third visit to lovely Walpole St Andrew. Despite the bitter wind of our first attendance at Walpole, I developed a liking for the area, with the fresh leaves on the hedgerows and the lambs gambolling in the fields, but on this particular year I took a dislike to the over-exuberant commentator. The steam show was finished but, as this was also Cup Final Day and I planned to watch *Match of the Day* on the caravan's television before heading for home, I was hurt when the the commentator bawled over the public address system: "And for any football fans . . ." then he proceeded to give the result.

I clapped my hands over my ears, but it wasn't enough to drown out the score. Half the fun of watching a football match is lost if you already know who is going to win!

In a distinct contrast to the open landscape of the Fens, our next show was in the heart of the City of London. A Doctor Burns who was organising the show had specifically asked me to bring *Ceōl* and *Prince* to a gala anniversary fair for St Bartholomew's Hospital, to be held in nearby Smithfield and the surrounding streets — but not in the meat market; that would be totally inappropriate.

I am forever thankful that we decided to arrive very early as the public turnout was simply amazing; from the outset there were queues waiting to get on the steam-driven gallopers, which would have been unusual even in the heyday of the travelling fairground. Very soon the organisers had to bring in portable railings to control the crowds.

We made lots of friends at that one-day event at Smithfield, and much of the time the crowds watching *Prince* were so dense that it was difficult for us to move around. The anniversary fair was a huge money-spinner for Bart's even though everyone came in free, and at the end of the day we were exhausted.

"Who said retirement is easy?" I asked Dee. "Whoever it was, he never owned a fair organ and a steam engine, that's for sure!"

The next outing was a simple organ-only local collection day for charity, which I managed on my own, then we had to prepare for two events in succession, with no opportunity to come home. The first was a big steam rally at Sellindge, between Ashford and Folkestone, in Kent. It was my first visit to this location but, after meeting Les Birch, a farmer and steam preservationist as well as the site owner and organiser, it was to become a regular call on our schedule; ironically, this was also to be the location for my last rally many years later.

The second event was only a few miles away at Hadlow Down, where we enjoyed meeting our old friends Claude and Joyce Jessett once again; I think I have more plaques from Hadlow Down than any other trophy — and for people who don't know, I should explain that every attendance at a major rally qualifies the exhibitor for a cast metal plaque as trophy. Now, a group of enthusiasts always made the Hadlow Down show something special, with displays of many facets of engineering. You could see them stripping down and overhauling traction engines, laying railway tracks, and looking after several big fair organs, plus a variety of other tasks destined to capture the public's interest. There were usually meetings in June and October, the autumn rally being mainly for organs; this was the time when the Harries Brothers brought their fairground amusements and gallopers and we all wallowed in nostalgia.

If I were ever to doubt the popularity of my attraction — a small-scale steam engine powering a fairground organ, the only such combination in the country — I need only look at the bookings to realise how much in demand we were. Our next engagement, for example, was with Enoch Doubtfire who had invited us to the impressively big Ripon Steam Fair, but we had allowed ourselves a little break between Sussex and the long haul up to Yorkshire.

Once more we gave ourselves plenty of time for the journey itself, leaving home on Thursday morning and arriving in the evening — but in daylight as we were now into June. Nonetheless, Dee had plenty to say about the experience: "It's not like driving a car, you know. That diesel Land-Rover with a caravan on the back is ruddy hard work. On the open road you've got to think a quarter of a mile ahead, and in traffic in towns you've got to think thirty feet behind, particularly when you're turning or passing parked cars. And as for reversing, don't mention it!"

As we unhitched the caravan and jacked it up, she could have added: "And now I've got to do the cooking!"

Ripon is a wonderful market town, where history is kept alive by the hornblower, a man in a tricorn hat and a bell, who sounds a horn each evening by the market cross, a tradition going back a thousand years. I was fascinated by the ninety-foot statue in the market which, they told me, was built in 1781 in honour of the man who was Ripon's Member of Parliament for sixty years. And then there's the Wakeman's House, now a museum. The wakeman was a night watchman who was paid by certain townspeople to guard their property. If they had anything stolen, the wakeman had to pay for it — an early form of household insurance. We explored the town and its immediate surroundings on the Friday and were ready for the show on Saturday and Sunday.

It was a great fair. I met a few old friends and made new acquaintances among other exhibitors, including Bill Ashley with his famous steam gallopers, a roundabout with a trumpet organ — an organ featuring trumpets, no less. Of course, there was no question that the Doubtfire gigantic firework display promised for Saturday evening held the crowds until darkness — around ten o'clock at night. After a hard day's organ playing with steam drive, the late night made us really tired, but we enjoyed it. And then we had to do it all again on Sunday — except for the fireworks — to even more spectators.

Sunday's people were extremely steam-minded; they would stand for ages watching *Prince* driving *Ceōl*. Peter Wilkes, a professional photographer, captured *Prince* at work, and this was duly published in *Model Engineer*. The crowds drained away in late afternoon and the fair closed soon after 5pm, allowing us an early night, as we wanted to be first away in the morning for the long drive home.

We didn't quite make it. Leon and Tania, acrobats who performed on a high, swaying pole and whom we often met on our travels, left the site just before us, on their way to an event in Norfolk.

We were home by Monday evening. We rested on Tuesday, then I took *Ceōl* to an organ-only do at Warley Hospital, Brentwood on Wednesday, and similar events on Saturday at Surbiton and on Sunday in Grays. Retirement? You must be joking.

A touch of oil keeps 'Prince' steaming steadily at the Horsham Rally.

THE NEXT OUTING was something altogether different. I can honestly say it was the best show that we ever attended in all our years on the rally circuit; it was one of the longest, as well.

I'll tell you how we happened to get involved.

A man who gave his name as Holden phoned me one morning to ask if I could bring *Ceōl* to Nuneaton, for a big exhibition that the Ford Motor Company was staging. "Would it be too far, or too long away from home?"

"It's not too far," I told him. "We've just come back from Ripon. But how long did you say?"

"Eleven days, starting July two, a Monday, until Thursday the following week, July twelve."

I hesitated. "That's quite a time." I facetiously asked whether the promoters could afford such a show.

"Don't fret about your fee, Mr Brooks. We just want you to be there."

My mind was already thinking of difficulties and alternative arrangements to make. "Right. I'll let you know within two hours," I promised.

So many problems to solve in so little time. If we went we would be away for much more than the eleven days as we were booked at Stratford-upon-Avon for the ominous Friday 13 July, then at Tewkesbury for the weekend of 21st and 22nd July — and we weren't planning on going home between Stratford and Tewkesbury as the sites were only thirty miles apart.

Allowing for two days travelling time, we would be away for twenty-two days. I asked Dee for her opinions, and she was agreeable, but we also needed her sister Irene for back-up driver and organ keyframe operator. Luckily she was at home when we phoned, and she agreed to help out. Nuneaton — here we come!

I received Ford's contract the next day, with a comprehensive itinerary. We set out on 1 July, well-loaded as I was carrying enough coal to keep *Prince* going until we reached Stratford. Food was no problem, as the caravan fridge was permanently well stocked and the womenfolk always found shops as only they know how.

We arrived in the afternoon to find the site was an old airfield and the Land-Rover and caravan would be parked by the former admin buildings. Using the skills I had picked up from professonal showmen I soon found an electricity socket to plug into for the fridge, television and lighting, which avoided the hassle of running the Land-Rover generator.

I said it was the best show we ever attended, but it was also one of the biggest. All that Sunday afternoon teams of workmen were putting the finishing touches to the displays and exhibits, many of them continuing long into the evening. It was to be a major display of Ford vehicles, mostly commercial, with numerous dealers manning their own stands. And somebody had even started digging a quarry to demonstrate the prowess of the giant earth-moving vehicles.

I was up and around early the next morning, enjoying the high summer sunshine. Soon I met the show manager who hinted that Ford had spared no expense in organising this exhibition. He told me to do whatever I thought best, and to enjoy myself. "There's a full lunch at the restaurant, and there's tea and refreshments on hand. Help yourself: everything is on the Ford Motor Company."

Obviously the vehicles were the main attraction, but there was plenty else to see, although we had the only organ and steam engine on display. I remember that beside us there was a baby elephant which everyone adored; he was only a little bigger than a sheep. He had plenty of room to move around inside his enclosure of straw bales but one night he managed to escape and caused more than a little anxiety until he was found.

I uncovered *Prince* around 10am and prepared to raise steam as the first visitors began arriving. The event was not open to the general public; entry was by invitation only, to dealers, customers, potential clients, and their associates, from around the world, which meant there'd be few children to admire *Ceōl* and *Prince*. Despite that, when the engine was in full steam and the organ was playing a variety of lively music, we soon had a small group of enthusiasts, asking all manner of questions. We had long realised that in the sixties and early seventies, many people had never seen or heard a fair organ since childhood: many, indeed, had never had the experience at all. What we lacked in children around *Prince* and *Ceōl*, we made up for with adults who were still children at heart — and that's most of us.

Among our enthusiastic admirers that first morning were some well-known television personalities. When Jimmy Ellis from *Z Cars* paused to look, I told him I was a great fan of his. He replied, studying *Prince*, "And I'm a great fan of yours!" He stayed around for quite a long time.

Later that day the big boss of the Ford Motor Company came to look at the organ and engine. I was stoking the fire at the time and as he studied *Prince* he commented: "This is the best thing in the show." Flattery, indeed! But I knew he was an engineer himself, and he understood the nature of steam engines. Ford's free lunches were of the quality one would expect at a five-star hotel, with a good selection of dishes, so I can return the flattery!

As the days passed we found that we were able to close down from 1pm until 2pm for some of those delicious lunches, with the show itself closing soon after 5pm; the exhibition did not open on the Sunday.

I said this was the best show we ever attended, so let me give you some idea of the attractions that were crammed into the afternoons of those ten show days. There were air displays on a big scale — we were, of course, on an old airfield — with my favourite being the bomber raids, with bags of flour for the explosives, and fighters coming in to the attack, all with the realistic sounds of warfare. There were medieval jousts with a big company of knights in armour astride beautiful horses; sometimes, I think, the knights got carried away in the excitement. And, this being a Ford promotion, there were displays of motor vehicles in all sorts of action.

Naturally, selling motors was the top priority, but it seemed to us as if everybody who was on the invitation list came to see *Ceōl* and *Prince* in action.

Some evenings, after the show had closed, I would take *Prince* off the trailer and drive around the site; the roads were ideal for this kind of activity and other exhibitors seemed to enjoy the engine's mobility more than its stationary efforts with the organ.

On other evenings we explored the country round about, taking advantage of the long summer days; we enjoyed Coventry, where the ruins of the Cathedral Church of St Michael, destroyed in 1940 by something stronger than flour bombs, stands beside the new cathedral designed in 1951 by Sir Basil Spence. We went to Leicester a time or two, and couldn't fail to notice the Gothic clock tower at the city centre. We were told this was built to commemorate four benefactors, the most important being Simon de Montfort, Earl of Leicester, who forced his brother-in-law Henry III to grant the first

English parliament in 1275. And, despite Mr Ford's generous restaurant, we sampled some nice ones in Nuneaton and Hinckley.

Our most memorable adventure was undoubtedly in Kidderminster Zoo where we went on the free Sunday, probably inspired by our neighbour the baby elephant, who normally lived there. Sister-in-law Irene was at the wheel of the Land-Rover, her later claim to fame being that she drove through Spaghetti Junction without getting lost.

We went to the monkey section first and were disappointed that only two animals were to be seen, and then at a distance. We drove on into the next field — and there were dozens of the little brutes, some of them leaping onto the Land-Rover and bending the aerial and windscreen wipers. I drove out as soon as I could.

Next came the big bears. I stopped to get a good view and one extra big animal came right up to the nearside door and stared at Dee, eyeball to eyeball. "Quick, Len! Drive on! If he puts a paw on the door handle it'll open! *Drive on, for God's sake!*"

She was nearly right: the door was secured only by a simple lift-operated lever. But from the safety of the driver's seat I consoled her: "You don't need to worry; bears are just inquisitive, but they'd push *down* on the door handle. In any case, you've got me to protect you." As Dee didn't seem to reply, I drove on. We had a great day at Kidderminster Zoo — I did, at least.

Cheryl Brooks helping with 'Ceōl' at the Knowl Hill rally.

The last four days of the great Ford show kept the excitement high right to the end; there was always something fresh to see. During our time there we received invitations to take *Ceōl* and *Prince* to several other events, including a Ford promotion at its Halewood plant to help promote a new model. I accepted.

We left early on Friday morning for the thirty-mile drive to the big steam rally and fair at Stratford-upon-Avon, organised by Harry Wigfield. Harry's shows were always first class and he invariably had the famous *Coronation Speedway* present. This was a fairground ride with motor-cycles instead of galloping horses, and it went faster. The pace of life at Stratford was quicker than at Nuneaton as we had children among the crowds — but we missed those Ford lunches.

After the rally we stayed on at Stratford to see the sights. And who would not: Stratford is England's second most important tourist attraction. We found it a beautiful place with its 15th-century half-timbered houses, some of them hiding beneath plaster façades added in Georgian times. Of course, the town's popularity originates with the boy who was born here around 23 April 1564, but it was the actor David Garrick who had the first Shakespeare Festival here two centuries later. The most famous building in the area must surely be Anne Hathaway's Cottage at Shottery, and I must admire the artists we saw capturing the picture on canvas with crowds milling around them.

Reluctantly, we left Stratford on Thursday morning, and arrived at Tewkesbury in the early afternoon as the rally was beginning to take shape; I noticed that quite a number of entrants had travelled long distances to be present. I met Roger Burville from Kent, with his beautifully-restored Mortier organ, and Bob Minney from Luton, who was showing his Imhofs organ built around 1850, and his Brüder of 1870, both of them pieces of great interest to organ buffs. I also met up with the Reverend Mr Miles with his big showman's loco-motive *Goliath*. I didn't need to ask his intervention for the weather that time as there was not a rain cloud in sight.

We opened on Friday and had three great days and, as my organ was the only one driven by steam, I had to answer lots of questions. Finally, on Sunday evening we were packing to go home; it was three weeks since we left Essex, but it seemed much longer. The journey itself was uneventful except for navigating the North Circular Road in London: how badly needed was that M25 motorway!

We had a few days rest before making our second visit to Tod Cody's New City Show at Milton Keynes, after which came the long haul north to Cromford, our first visit to this rally set in truly spectacular scenery.

Cromford is in the beautiful Derwent valley a mile or three south of Matlock, and is one of the villages where the Industrial Revolution began. Sir Richard Arkwright built the world's first mechanised textile factory here, using the 'spinning jenny' which he had invented; Arkwright's mill still stands beside the road, its walls built so thick that the unemployed hand-weavers could not force their way in and smash the machines that had killed their livelihood. Cromford, therefore, has a small part to play in creating the society which later built the steam traction engine, although we must thank Savery, Newcomen and Watt for developing steam power.

While we were at Cromford we naturally had a look at the sights, with the Crich Tramway Museum top of the list. This is in a huge chalk quarry that had been converted to an open-air museum by laying a considerable amount of track. By now, I understand, there are more than 40 trams at Crich, ranging from a steam tram built in 1885 for New South Wales, to *Glasgow 1297*, built in 1948 and in service for several years after that. The museum owners invited me to bring *Ceōl* to one of the open days, but I never did as I was always thinking of the chalk dust and its effect on the organ's pipes.

But you'll want to know about the rally itself? We played to an enthusiastic crowd on both days, and I met several other organ owners for the first time. I also made friends with the Howard Brothers, officials of the Cromford Steam Preservation Society and traction engine owners in their own right; they were later to acquire the famous Fowler showman's road locomotive *Renown*, quite a step up from their Marshall roller. And I met several model engineers — the Midlands and the North seem to abound in craftsmen — who were very interested in *Prince*; I learned that several were at the half-way stage in building, so it was obvious that *Prince*'s photograph and write-up in *World's Fair* had really started something. Naturally, I was bombarded with questions from the builders, and I had to confess again that I hadn't actually built *Prince*.

We started for home on Tuesday, but now that we were on the circuit there was little chance to take things easy. On Friday we set out for Knowl Hill near Maidenhead for that weekend's rally.

Knowl Hill has always been one of Britain's top events and I have received many cast-bronze medallions for attendance over the years but, regretfully, I missed the first one, which is now a collector's item.

The rally attracts many of the best organs and engines in the south, and in my days was ably managed by John Keeley and an active committee. Jimmy Williams always brought his travelling amusement fair, his steam-driven gallopers presented in first-class condition, a tribute to this craftsman with paint brush and spray gun.

At Knowle Hill I met up with Teddy Reed of Amersham and his helper, Norman Woodford, and I knew I could always get a hookup to one of the many showman's road locomotives for electricity — often to Jack Wharton's beautiful Fowler *Supreme*.

I think it's time I explained my set-up, as spectators were for ever asking me why I needed electricity if *Prince* were driving *Ceōl*? The truth of it was that *Prince* was only driving the bellows for the wind, and I had a small one-eighth horsepower *electric* motor to move the cardboard music through the keyframe. I also liked to light the inside and outside of the organ, as presentation was a major part of the fairground theme.

I could have devised some means of driving the keyframe with belting from the bellows counter shaft, but I considered the effort scarcely worthwhile as I still had to have electricity for the lights — and so, if I didn't get a hook-up, I had to run the Land-Rover engine to drive the alternator to provide the juice. To be brutally honest, it was the steam engine driving the bellows which was surplus to requirement as *Ceōl* could be — and often was — powered entirely by electricity.

One of the regular attractions at Knowle Hill was the unusual events, such as the old-time ladies' cycle race, with women in full-length Victorian dresses pedalling a range of machines, and there was usually more leg shown than the prim Victorians would have tolerated. But the most popular event was always the Cavalry Charge on the last afternoon, when every steam engine that was mobile — but not *Prince* as she was too small — raced down the field amid clouds of black smoke and hissing steam. The crowds loved it.

Now that we were a regular part of the rally circuit we had to face some tight schedules on several occasions. For example, we left Knowle Hill on Sunday evening, dropped *Prince*, the Land-Rover and caravan, at home, while Dee and I drove off in the Transit with *Ceōl* to be at the Aldeburgh Carnival by 9am on Monday.

Aldeburgh, pronounced *Oll-bruh*, is on the Suffolk coast, a charming town that seems to have escaped the hurly-burly of modern times. It was a busy port four centuries ago before coastal erosion began its work, and its famous Moot Hall, once in the town centre, now stands on the beach, defying the winter storms. Aldeburgh's most famous resident was Elizabeth Garrett, born in London in 1836 with strong ideas of a woman's place in society. When she married Dr Anderson she added his name to hers, an unknown action in those days, making her Elizabeth Garrett Anderson. She qualified as a doctor of medicine at a time when women were not allowed to study the subject, and she became Aldeburgh's mayor in 1908, the first woman in the country to hold that honour. Some woman! The town is probably more famous today for its annual music festival, now held at nearby Snape.

The carnival manager welcomed us as we arrived, and he sited us in a prominent position on the sea front with a convenient electricity socket nearby. Later, the manager asked if *Ceōl* could take part in the afternoon procession, still playing music. I had never done this before but the idea appealed to me; I said if somebody could find a small generator which could follow the Transit van, I thought it would work.

We played to a big audience until it was time for the procession. A small motor truck arrived with a petrol-driven generator aboard; I coupled my towing chain from the back of the Transit to the front of the truck and told the driver to keep the chain as tight as he could. The chain, of course, was a safeguard against letting the truck fall too far behind and so snap the power cable.

We started off, I at the Transit's wheel and Dee feeding the music into the keyframe. I had warned her not to venture too near the open rear of the van: I didn't want her to fall off. I drove in the middle of the road and took the corners wide on account of the trailing cable. I couldn't catch the music in the cab while we were moving in low gear, but each time we paused it was gratifying to hear the organ notes. At the end of the parade the carnival manager congratulated us, but I said that much praise must go to the truck driver as he never jerked the chain at all.

It was a wonderful and a memorable day, but as we headed for

'Prince,' mounted on her trailer, driving the bellows for 'Ceōl.'
(Photo: Peter Wilkes)

home down the A12 we had the sun directly in our face. We found the most agreeable answer to this little problem by pulling in to a roadside restaurant for an excellent dinner, and continuing the sixty miles home after dark.

We had just two days at home, allowing us to give *Prince* and *Ceōl* a good clean, and prepare the caravan and motors for the next mini-tour. And don't forget, I was supposed to be enjoying my retirement! The truth was obvious — I *was* enjoying it!

ON THURSDAY WE travelled to Caenby Corner, a small community due north of Lincoln where the Roman Ermine Street (now the A15) crosses the east-west A631. Immediately to the north is the oddly-named village of Spital in the Street. The Caenby steam rally was a well-established event, and the good road access meant that there were always plenty of traction engines. And that, of course, meant the specialist magazines had reporters and photographers in attendance, and so we were increasing our coverage in various pubications, particularly *World's Fair* and *Model Engineer*.

Friday morning. We thought we'd have a look at Lincoln and see if there was a suitable site for *Ceōl* on a future visit. We did some sightseeing as well — the ruins of the castle that William the Conqueror founded; the impressive cathedral, the third largest in England; and the Medieval houses in the city centre. There was a limit to what we could see in the time, so we missed the Guildhall where, they tell me, are swords given to the city by Richard II, Henry VII and Charles I.

But when we got back to the Land-Rover, it wouldn't start. *Don't fail us, I* begged, *all this way from home, and miles from our caravan!* I soon discovered that a heater plug had burned out so, to get the engine started, I short-circuited the dud. We found a Land-Rover agency in the city and soon had things set to rights — and we bought a spare plug.

The Caenby Corner rally was lively and hectic, and we rounded it off by a visit to Grimsby and Cleethorpes, purely as sightseers. And then we were off to the Bank Holiday show at the Royal Showground at Stoneleigh, south of Coventry. I needn't have touched the motorway in coming down from Grimsby, but I did — and I missed our exit. The next was one of those restricted-entry nightmares, so I pulled in at the Watford Gap services to take some refreshment and study the map.

As soon as we stopped an official-looking man approached us and announced: "Customs and Excise. I'd like to check your fuel, sir." As he tested the colour of our diesel oil with an impressive performance, he commented that 'some naughty farmers run on red' — that is, they use agricultural grade diesel which doesn't carry the taxes of derv, the fuel for diesel-engined road vehicles.

While we had a captive audience I told him we were lost and asked how far it was to the next interchange. He had already cast loving eyes on the tarpaulin covering *Prince*, which must have touched a sympathetic chord in his heart, for he said: "Just follow me." In his van he piloted us through a gate saying NO ENTRY, across a bridge over the motorway, and onto the northbound slipway. You know, at times there are distinct advantages in having a steam engine on tow.

The Royal Showground was on a huge expanse of land administered, at that time, by the National Agriculture Board. It was an ideal place for this three-day steam show, flat with nicely-mown grass, and there was even a stretch of water for the model steam boat enthusiasts. The show had its own extensive caravan site, away from the rally field, but I did not trust leaving *Prince* in the field where she was vulnerable to overnight theft, either on or off her trolley; the organ would be safe enough as I immobilised the Transit. Regardless of what the rules said, I therefore parked the steam engine beside the caravan just before dusk.

There had recently been a few thefts of 3in model steam engines, and I didn't want to be the first of the 4.5in victims. I was at an indoor exhibition when I heard that a 3in Burrell had been stolen by two men in brown overalls, looking very official, who lifted the model onto a trolley and boldly wheeled it away, no doubt to a waiting van. Now, the difference between a 3in and a 4.5in scale may not sound much, but it is significant — after all, the full scale engine weighs several tons. It would need more than two men to lift *Prince* and the getaway would have to be planned in much greater detail, but if a crime is technically possble, somebody will find the way to do it.

Later in the day I met Trevor Dawes the organiser, and owner in his own right of a steamroller in the course of restoration. He was pleased that I was able to attend — all the organisers said something like that, but it was nice to hear — particularly as I had brought *Prince*. In fact, *Prince* made me several new friends at the show, as well as renewing acquaintances already made at other rallies. It seemed to me that at Stoneleigh the best time for making contacts was while I was polishing *Prince*'s brasswork in the early morning sunlight, followed by the twisted brass canopy rods on *Ceōl*. Smartness and presentation are important in the fairground branch of show business, and I also had to keep a continual check on the light bulbs as we usually lost one or two in transit, more if we moved off before the filaments had time to cool down.

You'd like a tip for polishing brass? An old-time showman told me to use a stocking or pair of tights, and I can vouch that it works.

We played for the full three days of the show, then stayed for a few more days to visit several places of interest in the area, notably Kenilworth Castle. We learned that this fortress was built in 1112 in wood, but replaced by stone within the century. John of Gaunt added the great hall, Henry IV had the place as a royal residence, and Henry VIII built the chapel. But Oliver Cromwell ordered the castle be destroyed and it's now called the grandest ruined fortress in England.

Towards the weekend we hitched up and travelled the twenty miles to Hinckley, where we were exhibiting at a weekend steam rally which had quite a number of traction engines present.

We met two notable old friends at Hinckley. The first was Wilf Payne showing my old engine *Firefly*, which brought back many nostalgic moments, I can tell you. He generated the electricity for us, so saving the need to find a hook-up or run the Land-Rover. Wilf had put a lot of work into reroofing *Firefly*, and stripping the chrome off some of the brass twist — I had used the plated bars when I couldn't get plain brass.

On the Sunday we had a surprise visit from Walter Rasberry, who had travelled over from Norfolk purely to see *Prince*, the little steam traction engine he had built. If I felt nostalgic over seeing *Firefly* again, I can guess how Wilf felt over seeing *Prince*. He made a few minor adjustments, displaying all the love and fussiness of a mother with a newborn child, and I think I saw him wince when I told him the engine's usual stint was five hours of steaming, and occasionally eight hours, non-stop. Poor Walter!

We went home for a few days' rest before heading out for the next weekend rally at Horsham, a big show with steam engines from Kent, Surrey and Sussex, and several from further away. Each rally has its own memories, but what I recall most vividly about Horsham was the Saturday night. Most of us exhibitors were tired and had gone to bed, when we were rudely awakened by a fire bell.

Fire! But before we had time to gather our senses we heard the sounds of bawdy singing, and we realised there was no need to panic. The pseudo-firemen had taken the vintage fire tender on a pub crawl, and I suspect that several had taken far too much liquid aboard. Complaints followed in due course.

By now the summer was passing, and it was time for us to go to Roxton Park, Bedford: this was to be our third visit, and once again we were near the steam yachts which were always great crowd pullers. They weren't real boats, of course, but giant swings, such as the well-known *Shamrock*, and in my opinion they gave a stomach-churning ride. And after Roxton, we were to put in our first appearance at what was billed as the World's Greatest Rally.

STOURPAINE IS TO the traction engine and fair organ fraternity what the London Palladium is to variety artists, and the Old Bailey is to criminals. You are nobody unless you have been there. And now Dee and I were going to be 'somebodies' for I had spoken to organiser Michael Oliver on the phone and he had said we would be welcome. I suppose one could argue that I had talked him into inviting us.

It was a long haul to Blandford Forum in Dorset, and I found the Stourpaine site as outlandish and expansive a piece of ground as I have ever played upon. There were already lots of exhibitors when we arrived, some I had already met from as far north as Ripon. I knew from the number of entries on the programme that it was going to live up to expectations and be the biggest show, but I was already starting to worry. The soil was just a little muddy, and our Transit wheels, with the weight of *Ceōl* aboard, couldn't cope with heavy going. I decided to keep a weather eye on the western sky, in case of rain.

As soon as we were safely on the site I went to the office to book in, but the woman receptionist said: "Don't bother."

"But how will Mr Oliver know we've arrived?"

"Don't worry; he knows about everything and everybody that

comes here. I doubt that a stray dog would get past him."

Thus reassured, we found ourselves a pitch and set up shop for the three-day event, relying on Mike Oliver to find us when he felt so inclined. Despite this apparent highly-unorganised organisation, the rally was as much a success as I expected, and we enjoyed ourselves. The weather helped, too, allowing the ground to dry out somewhat.

Sunday was the big day, not only at Stourpaine but for us as well. The television people were there! The camera crew and the local news reporter saw *Prince* and *Ceōl* and were about to start filming when Michael Oliver appeared, so we were interviewed together — the owner of the biggest steam rally in Britain, and the retired paint manufacturer with the tiny steam engine driving a genuine fairground organ.

Fame at last, we joked afterwards. But there were more pressing things to think about: home. On Sunday evening I coupled up ready for an early start in the morning, but when somebody suggested we pull over nearer to the gate that night, I ignored his advice. I knew the travellers feared the notorious Stourpaine mud in those days but, in my abject conceit, I considered myself to be a good weather forecaster and I said: "No bother. It won't rain tonight."

After all, the stars were bright and there was no wind: why should it rain? I forgot that my meteorological experience had been built up in the dry east of England, and we were now in the wet west.

So how wrong can a man be? When we looked out the next morning I could only describe the scene as Southend when the tide is out: puddles and mud everywhere.

We really were in a panic now. We decided that Dee should get the Land-Rover out first; in four-wheel drive on its own it would have no problem, but it was towing a biggish caravan. I would follow in the Transit, with *Ceōl*. We knew we must not stop: we must move slowly and steadily towards the gate, working it so that we fitted into a slot in the traffic negotiating this solitary exit.

I had a final message for Dee. "Keep going, whatever you do. The Land-Rover shouldn't get stuck, but if the Transit does, wait for me down the road, far enough away to be safe. Best of luck, dear."

With tongue in cheek, I started to follow. Near the gate a few vehicles were negotiating the ground with difficulty, and a couple of burly men were pushing a car through the gap. Dee lumbered up behind and managed to slither through and onto the tarmac. I followed, sideslipping my way painfully slowly towards freedom — and I just made it, but at the expense of churning up the surface for vehicles following. I drove past Dee, flinging mud off the driving wheels, then we pulled into a convenient layby and had the panacea for all ills: breakfast, and a cup of tea. As we relaxed for a while, with only another 130 miles between us and home, I noticed a little hardening of attitudes as Dee said: "I never want to see Stourpaine again!"

I had to agree. In fairness, I must add that the rally has been relocated since then and I don't know what the new Stourpaine is like.

TWO DAYS LATER we were on our way to Liverpool to fulfil our obligation to the Ford Motor Company. We were, in fact, due at a Ford sales promotion project at Halewood, starting on the Thursday morning after Stourpaine and running through until Friday afternoon. From one point of view this was an easy booking as it involved just *Ceōl*, and gave us some spare time to take a ride on the metro buses and have a look around the city as the organ was not playing continuously.

From another point of view it was a difficult booking as we were due at a two-day steam rally in Paddock Wood, Kent, starting on Saturday. As soon as the Ford event closed we hit the road, and drove most of the night, arriving home in the early hours. We snatched a brief sleep before hitching *Prince*'s trailer onto the Transit and heading south once more, now with Dee driving the Land-Rover and towing the caravan.

We were home again on Monday, and managed to have a week or two of rest before setting out on the next jaunt, a mid-October visit to Beaulieu in the New Forest. Once again I was in the Transit with *Ceōl* and *Prince*, with Dee following in the Land-Rover, towing the caravan. We were nearing Winchester on the A33 — the M3 motorway had yet to be built — before I realised Dee was not to be seen in the rear mirror. The traffic was heavy and I had to travel a mile or so before I could pull off the road. I waited for her to catch up, then had to face the fact that she was not going to.

I couldn't turn at that spot because of the length of the trailer with *Prince* aboard, so I had to drive on for several miles, in increasing anxiety, until I could turn and retrace my route. Eventually I saw the Land-Rover and caravan pulled off the road in front of a cottage, and as I drew closer I could see the problem: the caravan was leaning. The nearside tyre had a puncture.

It was late on a Friday afternoon, not a good time to ask for help. Cursing myself for not carrying a spare, I started to jack up the trailer. I could see what was coming: Dee would have to stay and guard the Transit, *Prince*, and the caravan, while I drove the Land-Rover in to Winchester to get a new tyre fitted to the wheel. But just then a young man came out of the cottage and offered to help. He had seen the rally posters on the side of the Transit and was a bit of an organ and steam engine fanatic — just like the excise officer at Watford Gap.

"I'll run you in to Winchester with the wheel," he volunteered. But that was not all. He knew exactly where to go in the city, saving me much time and temper. Back at the roadside, he even helped me fit the wheel back on.

But where was Dee? As I took the jacks away from the caravan I realised she was nowhere to be seen. I was getting anxious about her when a woman called from the cottage to tell us that tea and biscuits were served, and we should come and join my lady wife.

What could have been a nasty incident had turned out to be relatively pleasant, and we had made more friends. After a short chat about traction engines and steam rallies I asked my Samaritan to accept payment for his services, but the most he would take was some postcards of *Ceōl* and *Prince*, and a closer look at the steam engine. We eventually arrived at Beaulieu just before dusk.

Beaulieu is pronounced 'bewley' but is really the French for 'beautiful place' — and it really is charming, an unspoilt village nestling on gentle hills between the forest and the Beaulieu River. This was our first time here, and I considered it an honour to be invited to the so-called Steam Happening at Lord Montagu's Motor Museum in the grounds of Palace House. Palace House, by the way, is the 14th-century great gatehouse of the Cistercian Abbey founded by King John. It is claimed that Margaret of Anjou, queen to Henry VI, and Perkin Warbeck, pretender to the throne of Henry VII, took refuge in the abbey — but not at the same time. Henry VIII had the place destroyed, leaving only the gatehouses.

On our first morning at Beaulieu we had a look at the abbey ruins and then visited the Motor Museum which holds a magnificent collection of cars and motor-cycles from the earliest days of motoring, and now even a Spitfire; Lord Montagu opened the museum in 1952 in memory of his father, an early car enthusiast. Most of the vehicles are in good working order and are often used in period television productions, and some of them are even subjected to the rigours of the annual London to Brighton rally.

I would have lingered longer with the galaxy of famous cars, but I had to light the fire and raise steam. Although I had no way of knowing it at the time, I was destined to visit Beaulieu on many occasions in the years to come.

With steam up and the organ in good voice, we played to a good crowd, although we were in competition with several big organs and engines, the showpiece being Beaulieu's own combination of the *Lady Hamilton* organ powered by the showman's road engine *Lord Nelson*. I think the attraction of our set-up was that the public could stand close enough to see the coal stoked into the fire, see the feed water pump supplying the boiler, and look right into the back of the organ to see the music cards going through the keyframe. It was quite by chance, but a feature of this arrangement was that one of us was always there to answer questions and chat to the enthusiasts.

I liked the special arrangement that Lord Montagu had made with the local church, where a Sunday morning service was being held: we would not play any organs until the afternoon.

We met several well-known people at Beaulieu over the years; I particularly remember talking to Dennis Wheatley, writer of thrillers and the macabre. Beaulieu must have been his inspiration for research into ancient vehicles.

Once we were home after that first visit to the Steam Happening, I found a spare wheel for the caravan, determined never to be caught in that situation again. But it was near the end of the season, and the caravan would not be used again that year; the final 'preservation event' was a one-day visit in the last days of October to mark the annual closing of the Sittingbourne Light Railway.

The SLR was around three miles long, linking Sittingbourne with Kemsley Mill on The Swale, the stretch of tidal water that makes Sheppey an island. The paper mill was formerly run by Bowater, the paper manufacturers who took it over from Kemsley Newspapers, and in the summer season an army of enthusiasts ran the light railway with clockwork precision. On this occasion we played *Ceōl* at the Kemsley end of the line and, as space was limited, we plugged into the mains for electricity.

The real outings, as I chose to call them, were over. Back home, we drained *Prince* as a precaution against frost, cleaned her inside and out, took her off the trailer where she was too vulnerable to theft, and sheeted her up. *Ceōl* still had work to do in collecting money for charity, but we stayed within our home circuit: Hornchurch, Watford, Romford, Billericay, Bedford and Brentwood. We were still in an era when there were few organs around and I like to think that *Ceōl* helped the fundraising in a material way because of her rarity value. But the best was definitely yet to come.

10: TROUBLES ON THE ROAD

DON'T LET ME give you the impression that life with *Ceōl* was always placid. It certainly wasn't. Travelling the country with an organ and a little steam engine always had its moments of triumph, of disaster, and of sheer comedy. Let me tell you some.

For a start, a few organ owners didn't want to play near what they called the 'smoky' steam engines, or they complained that the mud was troublesome. We old stagers just shrugged our shoulders and told them that this was what it was really all about and, anyway, there's always a tractor ready to pull them out. That's one of the nice things about a rally: one is never alone and there's always plenty of friendly help around. It's often a different story altogether at fêtes and minor shows, and even playing for street collections can sometimes be quite hazardous.

Take a sample year. Just after the football riots in Luton, I went to Watford with *Ceōl* for a charity collection, and noticed the heavy police presence.

"What's happened?" I asked.

"Nothing yet. We want it to stay that way, but Watford are at home to Chelsea today."

The police presence never slackened during the day and although the yobs swaggered around the town there was no real trouble. But the public stayed at home and the collection was £400 less than expected.

Not long after, I was playing in a sports and leisure complex in Shoreditch, London, on a Sunday afternoon when I heard a thump that made *Ceōl* shudder. I missed the incident but was in time to see a yob being escorted away by two burly lads in judo garb and black belts. They had the offender in a half-nelson and, with the help of two of their mates, they threw the yob out of the show, past a policeman watching passively.

It's often the places where you least expect trouble, that seem to have it. On another day at another booking a gang of punks with green hair, make-up, and the rest of their weird gear, started to harrass one of my collectors, and for a moment things looked critical. I picked up an iron bar — and I would have used it. My boxing days were long over, but I still had the fighting spirit. Well, those punks went right to the brink of provocation but then backed off. The bystanders, advised by the police not to 'have a go', stood idly by and watched, which is not so reassuring for anybody at the receiving end of trouble.

On the Saturday before Christmas I was collecting in the street with *Ceōl*. The clown and the other collectors, some in costume, were rattling their cans when three bovver boys came along, bent on making trouble. One of them confronted me by the organ and demanded collecting tins, saying they wanted to help. I refused to let him get on the Transit van, and called the organiser. This stopped the troublemakers, but only for the moment.

I switched from lively music to more sober carols as I know this calms down the more excitable people. It seemed to work on the bovver trio, but they went down the road, got tanked up on beer, and came back. Wihin minutes they were fighting with the collectors, but a van screeched up, police jumped out, and overpowered the trio on the muddy road.

One of the policemen smiled at me as they loaded the lads aboard the van. "They won't trouble you any more. They'll probably be our guests over Christmas."

I think the most frightening incident happened at Southend-on-Sea which, like other seaside towns, attracts more than its share of punks and offbeats. This was on a pleasant sunny afternoon, and I had noticed several patrons looking at the organ in a peculiar way. I got down to see why and, to my horror, a young man was standing there with a jagged piece of glass in his hand.

I said something like "What's all this about?" as I thought he was about to attack me, but there was something about him that suggested he was mentally or emotionally ill. He pointed to the proscenium and the situation crystallised: he obviously thought the carving of the busty wench had some religious significance.

I pleaded with him to give me the glass. "She doesn't want you to hurt yourself."

Leonard polishes the brass rods on the Transit van.

As he turned to me I saw he had already cut his face in two places, but at that moment a couple of policemen arrived, took him in a firm grip and with a "Come along, Terry," led him away. They evidently knew him.

That's enough of the macabre; let's have some laughs. One prank we still chuckle over happened at Pontin's Holiday Camp at Brean Sands near Weston-super-Mare. I was playing *Ceōl* there during a special week for model engineers and enthusiasts and met Pat Butcher and Fred Watson, both of them first-class model engineers specialising in traction engines. As we talked I suggested they put their models in front of *Ceōl* to make a smart display. You should know that Fred's model was a beautifully-finished showman's engine and a work of engineering art.

There were quite a few admirers when Fred went off to tea, with a request that we kept an eye on his model.

A few minutes later I said to Pat: "Tell you what: let's auction Fred's engine. What shall we start at — fifty pounds?"

Pat, who caught the glint in my eye, said: "I don't know if he'll take fifty."

I was then aware of two middle-aged women looking at the engine. One asked: "Is it really on sale for fifty pounds?"

"I'm not sure. The man who owns it has gone off for tea."

The women had another look at the model then went away, and I thought that was the end of it. But a few moments later we saw them coming back with a man. I hid behind the organ and Pat vanished in the crowds. The man, presumably the husband of one of the women, studied the engine and told them not to spend too much on it — less than fifty if possible.

Then we saw Fred coming back, and Pat drifted within earshot as the woman demurely approached Fred. "Are you the gentleman who's wanting to sell this engine?"

Fred was astounded. "Sell it?"

"We heard you were asking fifty pounds."

"Fifty pounds? *Fifty quid?*" Fred exploded. "That engine took me three thousand hours to make — three thousand! I've only just finished it and you can take it from me, lady, it definitely isn't for sale. Fifty quid, indeed!"

Some few weeks later I took *Ceōl* to play in Billericay, Essex, at a local charity. Historians and politicians may have heard of Billericay; it was here that Jack Straw led the Peasants' Revolt in 1381 protesting against the introduction of the poll tax in 1379, and where the Pilgrim Fathers met before going to Rotherhithe and boarding the *Mayflower* in 1620. And it's usually the first constituency to declare a result in a general election.

Everything had started smoothly on that day, and now the organ was playing and the collectors were jangling their tins. Then a serious-faced man with a short haircut and a smart shirt and tie asked me if I were in charge. I beckoned to John, the committee man, who came over. The serious one said we should stop playing for short intervals to give the nearby householders a break. John bristled. "I've got a permit," he said, pulling a paper from his pocket, "and I'm not stopping for anyone."

The serious one pulled out a card. "I'm Inspector Z and you're stopping for me. I'm closing you down for obstruction." As I was packing up the inspector told me in a more conciliatory mood that he would have allowed us to continue with just a few token intervals.

On another Christmas in the seventies I was taking *Ceōl* on the charity round, playing carols and traditional music. I had left Runwell Mental Hospital in Wickford, Essex, at noon after a morning session, and was due at Severall's Hospital, Colchester, in the afternoon. At that time Severall's was also exclusively devoted to mentally ill patients.

The main road was comparatively quiet around midday and I figured I had plenty of time to get to Colchester. Now, while it's an advantage to be early at most engagements, on this occasion it would mean waiting in the grounds and being overwhelmed with excited but well-meaning patients.

I slowed. The road was wide, the traffic light, and I was doing a comfortable 25mph when I saw a police car in my mirror. He overtook and stopped me, and the conversation that followed went something like this:

"Good afternoon, sir. May I ask why you're travelling so slowly?"

"I'm going to Severall's mental hospital and I don't want to get there too soon."

The policeman thought for a few moments, probably wondering if he had a joker or an escapee. "Where have you come from?"

"Runwell Mental Hospital," I replied with a straight face.

"And why are you going to the mental hospital?"

"To play an organ."

"Organ?" he queried. "What have you got in this vehicle?"

"The organ I'm going to play," I answered meekly.

"May I see your driving licence and insurance certificate?"

"I don't have them with me."

"How about your MoT certificate?" He could see that the Transit was far from new.

"I don't need one."

Now he was perplexed. "You don't *need* one? Really, sir, every vehicle over three years old needs a certificate."

"No. They excuse me."

"Oh, they do, do they?" He whipped out a book, wrote for a few seconds, and told me gravely to take my full documents to my local nick. Then, with a sympathetic voice, he suggested I drive slowly.

I was about to comment that that was what I was doing when he stopped me, but discretion ruled. The next day when I took my papers to the Harold Wood police station, I had my exemption letter from the Driver and Vehicle Licencing Centre at Swansea with me. But I decided not to reveal it just yet.

The desk officer examined the documents I showed, then asked for the MoT certificate.

"I don't need to have one," I said.

This policeman was more assertive. "All vehicles require a certificate, sir."

"Not if they have an organ fixed permanently in place," I answered.

The desk officer excused himself and sought higher authority, which happened to be an inspector who knew me from charity collections. "Ah! Mr Brooks. Yes, it's quite alright. Your vehicle is classed as an exhibition van and is not subject to an MoT test."

That was when I showed my DVLC letter. The inspector advised me to carry a photocopy of it and, in view of the circumstances, I thought it was good advice.

11: THE ABERDEEN RUN

THE FIRST OUTINGS of 1974, my second full year on the rally circuit, were town collections for charity, but on 24 March I was making my debut at Alexandra Palace. This was a big sale of bygones and other memorabilia, promoted by my old friend John Carter. I went to most of John's sales and I could see he was destined for bigger things; he had all the attributes of a first-class show director and I was not surprised when he became the proprietor of a steam fair.

There was even a time when I thought the car boot sale had developed from John's ideas, until I learned it had come over from the United States.

While at Ally Pally, John mentioned a big steam fair that he was planning for Blackbushe in Hampshire, set for a date in May. He wanted me to bring *Prince* and *Ceòl*, and as the date slotted in nicely, I agreed: the diary still had several large gaps in it. But I was not to know that this would be the beginning of one of *Ceòl*'s longest and most enjoyable tours, what I later referred to as the Aberdeen Run, even though it was only pure chance that took us that deep into Scotland.

On the due date late in May we prepared for a long stay away. *Prince* was loaded onto her trolley and secured; the caravan was well provisioned with everything Dee thought necessary to sustain us, and was hitched to the Land-Rover, itself fuelled and checked over. On Thursday morning we set out for the three-day Blackbushe Steam Fair, arriving early in the afternoon. The fair looked as if it would live up to its billing, for all of John's events were well organised as he was not hamstrung by committees and so could make snap decisions. Looking back on it, that event would cost a fortune to stage today, even if some of the rides were still on the road; one in particular was an old scenic gondola which eventually went to the Thursford Collection.

One never-to-be-forgotten exhibitor was our neighbour on site, the Romney, Hythe and Dymchurch Light Railway, which had been persuaded to relay some of its track and transport a steam loco from its base on the Romney Marsh. Now, who but John Carter could engineer that achievement?

Our next stop on the Aberdeen Run was to be at Chester, for the Cheshire County Show, but things didn't go according to plan. We left Blackbushe early and picked up the A34, the Winchester-to-Birmingham road, and were almost on the M6 on the eastern approach to Birmingham when I felt the Transit's clutch slip. Not wishing to stop in heavy traffic, especially with the Land-Rover and caravan following, I pressed on. I later realised it was a mistake, because the steep approach ramp to the motorway was almost too much, and I nursed the van up at little more than walking speed.

A mile or two along the motorway, a police patrol saw I was in trouble and stopped. I explained my predicament, saying that we were taking a fair organ to Chester, and once again I had struck lucky. Both policemen were interested in vintage shows, and they gave me the name and phone number of a Ford dealer. I used the emergency phone on the hard shoulder and was soon being towed in, quite slowly, to a motor workshop on a canalside near Walsall. Maybe the police knew something, for the depot manager and staff were interested in steam preservation and promised to have us in Chester by the next afternoon. They even allowed us to pitch the caravan in their yard.

The next morning, while the new clutch was being fitted, I polished *Prince* and *Ceōl*, as a sort of running entertainment for the mechanics. We were on site at Chester by early evening, and before dark we had dined and rigged up everything for Wednesday's opening.

The show was a great success from our point of view as there was still the novelty of a small steam engine powering an organ. *Prince* steamed non-stop for seven hours, and we were all featured on Granada Television's local news that evening. The second day was not so enjoyable because heavy rain made the driving belt slip, so I decided to power the organ from the Land-Rover, which went completely opposite to what had been featured on the previous evening's television! And I dread to think what it would cost now to run the Land-Rover all day to generate electricity.

Despite the rain, the crowds were thick all day and, although I grumbled about the weather, everybody was agreeing that the rain was desperately needed. Indeed, that was about the time of the great drought. The skies cleared late in the afternoon and we were able to pack up without discomfort, ready for an early start the next morning.

If you ever exhibit at a county show, or any event of comparable size, always be ready to get away as soon as possible — particularly after rain — as the large vehicles involved in dismantling the major stands frequently cause delays around the exit. Having learned this from experience, we managed to cover the 85 miles to our next stopover with no problem, arriving at Levens Hall around 12.30.

I must explain that Levens Hall is a beautiful Tudor mansion at Levens Bridge, five miles south of Kendal, Cumbria. Inside, the house is famous for its leather panelling, its chimney-pieces, and the ornate plaster ceilings, but we never had the opportunity to see these. The large grounds have a wonderful display of topiary, originally designed by the man who relaid the gardens of Hampton Court three centuries ago.

Alf Lamb, the man in charge of the site, met us as we pulled in, and he was delighted when I offered to play in Milnthorpe, two miles down the road, on Friday afternoon to advertise the rally. The event itself, organised by the Morecambe Bay Traction Engine Club, was first class. I met several old friends, the weather was good, and there were many fine organs and engines on view — but my *Prince* was still high on the popularity lists.

Among the new friends I made was Bill Dorman of Nottingham touring with his steam gallopers. He added that he and his party were going on to the Bon Accord Rally at Aberdeen after Levens, then threw me the challenge: "Why don't you come as well? It's a great rally, and they'd love your organ and engine. Tell you what — I'll give you Bill McConnachie's number and you can ask him yourself."

Aberdeen? We were miles from home as it was, but Aberdeen was 250 miles away, and in the wrong direction. Dee and I talked it over and quickly made up our minds to give it a go. That evening I rang Bill McConnachie, and committed ourselves.

But we still hadn't finished with Levens Hall. My small steam-driven outfit was very popular, and the rally was a success until an hour before we were due to close on the Sunday. That was when the heavens opened in a typical Lake District downpour. It didn't rain for long, but the ground became so saturated that the engines and other heavy rally traffic churned up the field. It was my first rally at Levens Hall, but it was everybody's last, as the owner of the museum vowed he would never be host to another mudchurning event.

We stayed in the area for the next two days, touring this beautiful corner of England and visiting Morecambe Bay, whose vast low-tide sands are known locally as the 'wet Sahara'. On Wednesday we set off for the north, through Carlisle and across the lonely but spectacular Cheviots. We reached Edinburgh in the early afternoon but had no opportunity to explore this historic city, then we crossed the Forth Road Bridge. We were really tired by the time we reached Perth in the early evening.

We decided to try a rather up-market touring caravan site, so we left the Transit van and *Prince* outside and drove up to the site office in the Land-Rover, with the caravan on tow: experience had taught us that some site wardens didn't like to see the flamboyant posters on *Ceōl*'s van. After we had booked ourselves in I casually mentioned that I was taking a vintage organ to Aberdeen, and I dropped a few names to impress.

"Of course it will be alright! Put it in the car park; it'll be safe there." I shall never know if we'd have been so welcome if the warden had seen the van first.

We didn't start out quite so early on Thursday as I estimated we had only around 80 miles to go, and yesterday's hills had given us no problem. We followed the coast through Dundee to Stonehaven, with a mere fifteen miles between us and Aberdeen. And there we found a frighteningly steep hill. I don't know whether it was the fear of clutch trouble again, but that hill really had me worried. I was soon in bottom gear and after what seemed an eternity I pulled in to a layby; I ran back to Dee grinding up in the Land-Rover and suggested we have a cup of tea while the engines cooled and we worked out a strategy. I was considering uncoupling *Prince*, driving the Transit to the top of the hill, then using the Land-Rover to bring up the caravan and *Prince* on separate runs. But when I walked up to the summit I was surprised to find we had only a matter of yards to go.

We arrived in Aberdeen early in the afternoon and soon found Hazelwood Park, the site of the Bon Accord Rally.

It was a perfect location, and the fairground was nearly built up — that's showman's language to say the fair was nearly assembled. Later we met Bill McConnachie and his fellow committeemen — and what a welcome they gave us! We spent the Friday seeing some the city sights, including the cathedral, the outside of the 15th-century University, and the medieval quarter; it whetted our appetite for the other attractions of the area, starting with Balmoral Castle, but we had no time.

When we returned to Hazelwood Park the show was almost ready, and we could feel the atmosphere of expectation and anticipation that spells forthcoming success. The last of the exhibitors arrived late in the evening, but at latitude 57 and-a-bit north in high summer, it doesn't really get dark at all.

Saturday dawned as another glorious midsummer day. I remember waking to the skirl of the bagpipes and savouring the thrill of having brought *Ceōl* and *Prince* this far north, and on the threshold of some

A beautiful study of 'Prince' in action.

of the grandest scenery in the United Kingdom. But duty called, and we spent the morning cleaning the organ, polishing the engine, and preparing for firing-up. *Prince* was the centre of attraction among our fellow exhibitors as we belted up the wee engine to the organ: I doubt if anybody in the Scottish Highlands had ever seen a steam engine that small.

The Bon Accord opened at noon, and the visitors came in their *thousands*. The engine steamed for seven hours and *Ceòl* played non-stop: it was one of the most satisfying show days we ever had, and the weather stayed perfect. Sunday dawned equally bright — we had always been led to believe it rained a lot in Scotland — and if we thought Saturday's attendance had been good, by two o'clock on Sunday afternoon it seemed as if half the population of Scotland was there. I had so many folk around me that I had difficulty in stoking and watering the engine.

That evening, after we were packed up and ready to move out, we were dog tired but thoroughly happy. I wandered past Bill Dorman dismantling his gallopers. "Glad you came?" he called.

"Fantastic! I wouldn't have missed it for worlds!"

"Good! See you around!"

Bill was going on to The Netherlands while we were beginning the long haul back to Essex, with a chance to explore Edinburgh and with more rallies to visit on the way. But we never saw Bill again and he is now playing those great gallopers in the skies.

We woke very early on Monday to that dreaded sound of rain beating down on the caravan roof. Looking out, I could see puddles forming on the grass, and I knew we were heading for trouble. I threw on some clothes and drove the Transit, with *Prince* on tow, onto hard ground. Although the van had double rear wheels, traction was difficult in wet conditions with a heavy trailer in tow, and I only just managed it, the ground breaking up under us. We had an early breakfast and got away: there was no immediate urgency to move the caravan as the Land-Rover's four-wheel drive and low ratio could pull us out of almost anything, as we had already proved at Stourpaine.

And so we began the homeward leg of the Aberdeen run. The hill at Stonehaven gave us no problems in this direction, and we drove on through the rain, which stopped as we reached the Forth Road Bridge: Scotland was living up to its reputation after all.

We had been recommended to try a certain caravan site near the bridge. It was council-owned so once again I left *Ceōl* on the road while I walked in to negotiate. As it happened, the warden liked vintage vehicles and welcomed us inside; he was delighted when I gave him pictures of *Ceōl* and *Prince*.

While we relaxed that evening, I reflected on the Stonehaven hill and thought how close we had come to serious problems, if not disaster: we could have ripped out the new clutch, or ruined the engine by demanding it do the impossible. After all, I was asking the Transit to do far more than it was designed for. The organ and its music were heavy, there were two large electric motors, two spare wheels, lots of tools, usually a box of coal, and almost always something hitched to the towing-knuckle: if it wasn't *Prince*, then it was the caravan. The answer was obvious; the small four-cylinder engine must go, and be replaced by a more powerful V-six.

Back home after the Ripon rally, I began making inquiries about a replacement motor and found myself directed to a small repair shop run by two excellent engineers. They agreed that I was flogging the Transit engine to death, and suggested I look for a good V-six diesel motor from an insurance write-off, as a new engine would cost too much. They told me they had done several such jobs, and they would need to replace the front of the vehicle, including the radiator, as a diesel engine was much larger. And it was up to me to find the motor.

I called my friend Phil Ives, who ran a large breaker's yard as well as being a lover of traction engines, and he promised to keep an eye open for what I needed.

Meanwhile, we were back on the road, with two fairly easy outings, to Netley Marsh near Southampton, and the Town and Country Show in Brixton. The Brixton event was always well-organised and in those days there was never a hint of the riots that were to follow; in fact, the exhibitors slept in their caravans parked near what was later to be called the Front.

The replacement engine had not yet come to light — we were waiting for the mechanical equivalent of a heart transplant, which depended upon a suitable donor being found. So we set out on our next tour with just a little trepidation, as we were heading north again, where hills were hills, and they never let one forget it.

We revisited Cromford in Derbyshire, then paid our first visit to

Castle Howard in North Yorkshire. It's not really a castle: to my way of thinking it's a palace, and I was to learn it's the largest stately home in all the Yorkshires — no wonder it's used for locations in so many films and television programmes.

I learned something of its history, too. The old Henderskelfe Castle was burned down in 1693, so the 3rd Earl of Carlisle ordered this vast mansion to replace it. But he chose a Sir John Vanbrugh as architect, which was strange as Sir John was a playwright and an officer in the marines, and only an amateur at architecture. Sir John chose Nicholas Hawksmoor as his assistant and clerk of the works, and *he* had worked with Sir Christopher Wren, architect of St Paul's Cathedral.

Building began in 1700 and took 37 years to complete, at a cost of £78,000, an incredible sum in those days when you could buy an ordinary cottage for around £25. Neither Hawksmoor nor the earl lived to see the house completed, but Vanbrugh made himself such a reputation that he went on to build Blenheim Palace.

The house has been open to the public for years, and we enjoyed seeing some of the incredible display of furniture, pottery, paintings and statues, by artists of world-wide fame. It was just too much to appreciate in one visit, particularly as we were there in the thousand-acre park to play *Ceōl* in the Great Yorkshire Steam Fair.

While we were in that part of the country we took the Monday off to visit Scarborough in the Land-Rover, but we came away with the impression of a vast and beautiful beach littered with fish and chip wrappers. I know it has changed since then. The rest of the town was attractive, particularly the cleft which splits the community in two, and the ruins of a castle clinging to a clifftop several hundred feet above the sea. Spectacular! On Tuesday we toured the Dales, then on Wednesday we headed south again for Caenby Corner and another visit to Stoneleigh, south of Coventry.

The season was nearly over. We took *Prince* and *Ceōl* to steam events at Roxton Park, Bedford; Henham Hall, near Southwold in Suffolk, which I shall discuss later; Hadlow Down in Sussex; and the closing of the light railway at Sittingbourne, Kent. Then we were left with the organ-only charity events nearer home.

I was yet to realise it, but there were to be some major changes in the coming season.

12: TELEVISION DEBUT

THE ARAB WORLD decided it wasn't getting enough money for its one major export, oil. The newly-formed Organisation of Petroleum Exporting Countries, OPEC, doubled the price of a barrel of crude, and promised yet more increases. The result was catastrophic in the industrialised world: queues formed at gas stations in the USA and the makers of the enormous and inefficient gas-guzzling automobiles found they couldn't sell their products. Japan, totally reliant on imported oil, was facing economic ruin but countered by developing the compact car, soon to dominate the market. And Britain issued petrol coupons in anticipation of rationing. Here, the price of a gallon rose from forty of those new pence and everybody knew it would soon pass the pound mark.

On the immediate front,.I would never again consider letting the Land-Rover engine run all day just to generate electricity, and I would need more expenses before travelling long distances. It was the start of the first big surge in inflation that made millionaires out of property speculators, and paupers out of fixed-income pensioners.

Early in that year, 1975, I had given *Ceōl* a facelift with new gold leaf, and Victor Chiappa had paid his annual visit to tune the organ ready for its first appearance at Easter. The first full steam rally was at Merton in south London, then we were off to Walpole St Andrew again. Before the rally opened to the public I was driving *Prince* under full steam around the site when I met Wilf Payne with my old engine *Firefly*, and talked him into powering the lights for me from his dynamo. A little later Walter Rasberry found us and began amusing himself nostalgically with *Prince*. I should have recognised the signs.

Later in the afternoon Walter strolled over to our pitch. He made small talk then came to the purpose of his visit. "Would you consider selling *Prince*?"

"Sell her?" I was surprised and a little shocked. "Not really. I'd be very reluctant to part with her . . ."

Sell *Prince*? She was an integral part of my exhibition, although she wasn't strictly essential. But why should I agree to sell her? In a moment of weakness I answered deviously: "It would depend on the price and whether you caught me in a moment of weakness. Anyway, who wants her?"

"Wilf would like a miniature engine and he wants me to build him one, but I'm too old to go through all that again."

Wilf. Well, if I sold *Prince* to Wilf, she could scarcely be going to a better home, I conceded to myself, and that was my moment of weakness. I was reluctant, reticent, hesitant, but as I was among friends I found it impossibly difficult to refuse. Before the rally was over Walter had negotiated the price, and it was Wilf who hitched up the little traction engine and took her to her new home in Norfolk.

I was sorrier after selling *Prince* than I was after selling any other engine, and Wilf's widow, who now owns the miniature Burrell, tells me: "I'll never part with it. It's no good you trying." She has the strength of character that I lacked at the vital moment.

With *Prince* gone, I was now an organ-only operator, but I was pleased to note it didn't make any difference to the number of events I was asked to attend, although the most prestigious invitation came quite unexpectedly.

I HAD RETURNED home after one of my solo mini-tours and was relaxing when Dee said, almost as an afterthought: "By the way, the BBC has been on the phone. The man said something about maybe wanting you to go on the telly."

I laughed. "Stop kidding. What would they want me for — the Benny Hill Show?"

"Here's the phone number; why not find out?" Indeed, the number looked impressive enough, with a four-digit extension.

Sure enough, it was the Television Centre, and the girl who answered the extension number said the producer wanted to speak to me. As the seconds of waiting ticked away I began to feel quite excited. Then: "Hello, Leonard. I'm Albert Barber, producer of *Playschool*." A few pleasantries, followed by: "Look — we're searching for a fair organ to appear in an episode of *Playschool*. Would you be interested?"

Would I be interested? Can a duck swim!

"Y-yes," I stammered. "When would you like to see it? The day after tomorrow?" This, I thought, would give me a day to clean it; after all, I had just come back from a rally and the caravan was still hitched up.

"Can't wait that long, I'm afraid. Could we see it tonight? I'll come down to you; it'll only take an hour."

I didn't need any persuasion to yield. I knew that producers were men in a hurry and this venture was *go* from the start. "Okay. Is eight o'clock alright?" and I gave him directions.

I unhitched the caravan, plugged *Ceōl* into the mains, and cleaned up a little at the back. There was no time for a polish, but the machine would still look quite nice with the lights on.

Almost on the dot of eight Albert Barber and his assistant pulled up outside. Soon I had them in the lounge and was showing them press cuttings and photos of *Ceōl*; Albert explained that he was looking for an organ that had movement, lights and, of course, must sound correct. I assured him that *Ceōl* had all these qualities, then led him out to see for himself. As it was nearly dark I switched on all the lights before unlocking the front flaps, and the effect was quite startling with the sudden flood of illumination against the black background.

I started playing the *Petite Waltz* and both visitors were delighted with the whole scene. Albert said he liked the tune so much that he would have it in the programme — and that told me he had already decided to use the organ. Straight away we began a kind of rehearsal, timing the music and deciding where to start and stop, when and where to re-start, and so on, all done precisely to the second with a stopwatch. I marked the music card with all this information, and the pauses. Then they measured the Transit van, as it had to go in the studio.

Albert gave me a copy of the script — they had already written it! — saying casually that I would find my lines inside. "You mean I've got to speak on the programme?" I asked, almost in horror.

"Don't worry, Leonard. There's nothing to it. In any event, there'll be plenty of rehearsals before we go live." All I had to do, he added, was follow the presenter's lead. I hoped the date wouldn't clash with any other arrangements and, as if sensing my concern, Albert asked: "Can you be at Wood Lane next Wednesday at two o'clock sharp?

You'll get all the paperwork in the next day or so."

They finished by taking a few photographs: the one of me at the keyframe is the one used for the cover of my record album — I'll tell you about that soon. And then, with a quick farewell, they were gone and as I closed the organ I was left to ponder what I had let myself in for.

Over supper I studied the script but I couldn't see any set words for me to say. Instead, there were instructions such as *Leonard turns to Lionel and explains how the organ works.* When I thought about it, that was the best way to do it: I knew what to say, and I would say it in my own words. But *which* words? It would be fairly easy to explain to adult viewers, but how would I put it over to young children without losing their interest? My other 'lines' seemed to offer no problems at all, and the large package of instructions which the BBC posted me, were straightforward. I had to concentrate on just two points: put the message over simply, and be there by 2pm.

Wednesday. I was up early, and pleased to see it was a fine day. I gave *Ceōl's* brass an extra shine, tidied up, and was on my way. Knowing that Wood Lane and the television studios were an hour and a half's drive away, I allowed three hours, just in case.

I arrived at the studios a little after 11.30 and, after I showed the commissionaire my pass and letter of authority, he directed me to a large car park. I was amazed at the vast size of Television Centre and it was quite a while before I found the right studio. They were recording another programme but a *Playschool* technician was found to help me. He was interested in the prospect of the organ coming inside, and we were soon talking about fairs and steam rallies. "There's plenty of time," he assured me, "the studio won't be ready until two o'clock." But the clock ticked on, wasting valuable moments I was soon to need.

Near the two o'clock deadline I reported to another official who would make the arrangements for escorting my vehicle through the corridors to the studio. He asked casually: "You got much petrol in the tank?"

"About six gallons."

"Oh-oh," he grunted. "It's got to come out. You're only allowed a pint — fire regulations."

Time was ticking away towards two o'clock. "Do you have a drum? I'll siphon it out."

"Sorry, sir. Can't do that on the premises. You'll have to go to the service station in Wood Lane; they'll do it and charge the BBC."

Why hadn't somebody told me that earlier? To reach the garage I had to negotiate a lengthy one-way system; then the foreman wasn't happy with the arrangement, grumbling about the amount of paperwork involved, and the months before they got paid. And the clock was ticking on: it was already past 1.30.

"Can you sell me a five-gallon drum?"

"Sure. But you can't draw off petrol on the forecourt . . ."

"I know: fire regulations." So I parked a little way up the road and did it, which was probably more dangerous because of the passing traffic. Then when I'd drained off most of the petrol, I still had it — in the can!

Back to Television Centre, the commissionaire, and more delay, this time because *Top of the Pops* was being recorded and the fans were trying to get in to see their idols. The gates were closed, and the security men were chasing youngsters away; some had even scaled the walls. Eventually I got in and threaded my way through a maze of lorries and scenery trucks to the appointed doorway where I met Albert Barber. "Glad you managed it in time," he said breezily, as if I had just arrived instead of having been there two hours already. He left me in the care of the floor manager, to whom I explained the problem about the petrol. He solved it by buying the drumful from me and putting it in his car — a few minutes before 2pm.

Then I drove into the studios, a tricky manoeuvre down a long corridor past hand trucks laden with scenery, through the door into the *Playschool* studio, then gently manoeuvring into the exact position. I came down from the driving seat and looked around at my audience of technicians, and forgot all about those 'butterflies in the stomach.' The electricians had a good laugh at my antiquated direct current switch and meters, but I assured them that *Ceōl* was quite at home on 230v AC.

"Nevertheless, I think we'll have a safety earthing transformer in circuit just to make sure," one of them smiled.

As soon as the organ was operational there was a clamour for a tune; I had to test it, anyway, so I put on a stirring march. It sounded really magnificent as the acoustics were perfect.

Now it was time for rehearsals. Albert Barber came with the

117

presenters and he introduced me to them: Lionel Morton, better known from *Jesus Christ Superstar*, and Sarah Long. "And are we all familiar with the script? How about you, Leonard?"

"Not quite. I'm a bit worried about explaining how the organ works. I don't want to get too technical . . ."

Albert handed me over to Lionel. "You two can work it out between you; all your speaking parts are with Lionel." He patted my shoulder. "Good luck, Leonard, and don't worry: you'll do fine."

I explained my problem to Lionel. "Do I start with the bellows or the music cards? How much do you think I ought to say about air pressure and regulating the speed . . . ?"

"I see your point," Lionel agreed, then he picked up the music book, let a few cards fall through his fingers, and said, as if to the camera: "You've heard the organ. This is the music. Funny music, isn't it? It's full of holes. It's the holes that make the notes." With a smile he handed me back the book. "That's all they'll want to know. And keep your sentences short."

It was fascinating to see all the studio work that goes into making a simple television programme — and that's without the planning and research. I knew that *Playschool* ran for just 25 minutes on air, and I thought we'd be away in a couple of hours, but when I

Sarah Long and Lionel Morton with 'Ceōl' in the 'Playschool' studio. (Photo: BBC Television)

mentioned this to one of the technicians he grinned. "We'll be lucky to be away by eight."

The theme of this progamme was to be musical boxes, hence the need for *Ceōl*. The first run-through seemed to be separate little sketches, often repeated for different camera angles. Then at last my turn came. The floor manager came over with Lionel and explained what I had to do; we repeated our parts a few times for fluency. "Don't worry," Lionel advised. "And don't rush it; this time it's not for real." He paused, then: "And this is Leonard who has brought his magnificent organ into the studio . . ."

I said: "I'll be delighted to play it for you . . ." I ran *Ceōl* for a little while, looking for the mark on the music card so I could stop it for a bit more dialogue. But we ran into a problem. *Ceōl* cannot shut down dead like a switched-off radio, and when I stopped the music the air power was still on. A technician came over and grumbled: "We can't have that background motor noise; it's picking up something awful."

We tried again, this time with one hand on the air switch and the other on the music drive switch. But at the stop mark we got a fading chord as the reservoir emptied. I looked at the sound man and saw we still had a problem; I hadn't needed to worry about refinements like this at the rallies. Then the answer came: "Let's do it again, and lend me someone to switch the motor off." I gave simple instructions to my new assistant: "Turn off when I nod." And as we switched off together, I slipped a piece of cardboard under the music, which blocked the air. The tune stopped on the instant, with no fade.

I continued the rehearsal with my next piece with Lionel, but before we could break for a snack, the clock scene had to be done. This was an integral part of *Playschool* every day: "The small hand is on four and the big hand is on twelve. It's four o'clock." The snag was that the clock kept striking five!

After the tea break we did a more sophisticated rehearsal — at least, the organ never played better — and then we broke for dinner. "The next take is for real," Albert warned. On our return to the set there was a discernibly different atmosphere building up, which was heightened when a charming woman from the make-up department called me over. "Come on, my dear; it's your turn." I didn't expect the full treatment of powder and cosmetics and when she saw I was flustered she explained. "It's quite OK. Everybody has to have make-up. Without it those lights would make you look terrible."

Soon we were all in our places, with batteries of strong lights beaming down at us, and huge cameras on mobile pedestals manoeuvring around us. I was expecting the entire programme to be shot in one sequence, starting at the beginning and going through to the end, but it didn't happen that way. While I stood at the back of the organ, watching the recording and waiting for my cue, Lionel gave me some little last-minute reassurances. "The main thing is, speak up, and don't hurry," he said, "and you'll do fine."

He warned me when my time was coming up, and I must say the interview seemed to go smoothly. I told the young viewers how *Ceōl* worked, answered a few more questions, and then we played the music. With help on the switches the organ stopped dead on cue, and without any fade. Then came the clock scene, and it chimed five once again, but Albert told me later that they'd cut the last chime off the sound track. We all assembled in front of *Ceōl* for the finale, and the recording session was over. Everybody said how pleased they had been with the organ, and I found myself invited upstairs to the hospitality suite, but I was keen to get home — and I had to fill my petrol tank. As I manoeuvred the Transit out of the studio and back towards the real world, I called out: "Thanks! It's been one of *Ceōl*'s best outings!"

I was delighted with the recording when it was transmitted a few days later; all the separate bits had been edited to perfection and, watching it, I felt I would have liked to go back and do it all again. Indeed, that's what happened some while later.

AFTER THE TELEVISION show, we did two local events and then went south to Sussex for the Ardingly Steam Rally and the Polegate Steam Show. Polegate in particular was a friendly rally, the whole show managed by Arthur Handmore and his wife, a lovely couple who did their job well. The problem was the nasty accident that occurred here.

I suppose it was one of those incidents just waiting to happen. The latest craze was for radio-controlled model aircraft, and all was going well, with the models doing virtually everything a full-scale machine can do, until a large model went out of control and dived straight into the crowd. The air display was stopped within seconds

120

and a St John ambulance took a man to hospital.

Rumour was rife, but we all knew that the man had been badly injured. Later, when I asked at the official tent, I was told he was in intensive care. I heard a model-club official try to explain the incident with the possibility of a police or other walkie-talkie having come in on the same wavelength and interfered with the controls. The last I learned was a newspaper report which said the victim was still seriously ill.

WE DID THE usual run of rallies through the autumn and finished the year with the charity collections, visiting eight towns.

Phil Ives found a good second-hand six-cylinder diesel engine for the Transit around the end of January of the next year, 1976, and I made arrangements to have the change done on the first Monday in March with Tuesday a spare if needed.

And then the BBC asked me to go to Manchester for another *Playschool* recording on Thursday — which meant I would have to set out on the Wednesday. The schedule was tight, so I contacted the mechanics to impress how important it was to keep to time.

They grinned. "Don't worry, Len; you didn't tell us you were a TV star! We won't let you down."

As it happened, I collected *Ceōl* on Tuesday morning, with the instructions to drive gently for the first 500 miles. We spent the rest of the day getting the caravan ready, for this would be a three-day trip and Dee was coming to see the fun. I turned out most of the cardboard music, and anything surplus to our needs, while Dee made up the lost weight by stocking up with food, plenty of warm bedding, and suitable clothes. We hitched up for an early start.

Wednesday dawned cold but bright. We headed across the north of London for the M1, a tiresome drive with numerous traffic lights — I wish there had been an M25 in those days! It normally took an hour and a quarter to reach the motorway but, due to the need to nurse the engine, we added thirty minutes to our time.

We stopped at the Teddington Services, having covered 50 hard miles; we checked the engine and had a snack before continuing to the Watford Gap services and another break. Traffic was heavy on the M6 to Birmingham and there were long lane closures, so by the time we reached the Hilton Services we knew we would be driving in Manchester after dark.

In fact, we hit the city in the rush hour, which made it difficult to stop. But I had to pull up to ask the way to the new studios near Oxford Road. I turned into a sidestreet and asked the ideal person, a passing postman. Despite his thick Irish accent I *think* his instructions came down to 'right, left, and right.' We tried it, both of us looking for suitable buildings, but without luck. Then I saw another postman and hopped out of the van to ask again.

"I just told you!" he cried, then repeated it slowly as if he were talking to somebody with a learning difficulty. This time we followed his words meticulously, and arrived at the locked gate to a car park. I left Dee in charge while I scoured on foot — and learned we were at the studio's rear entrance: the postman had sensibly not sent us to the front, where parking was impossible, but he hadn't know the gate was locked. I showed my papers at the main entrance, got the gate unlocked, and we drove in, finding a sheltered spot for the night.

We were up and breakfasted just after 8am I gave the Transit a good rub down, particularly on the presentation side, checked *Ceōl*, and we were ready. With signs of activity appearing in the studios, I found Albert Barber who was directing the programme; in fact, it was almost the same team I had met in London. He gave me my

"To Leonard, with love from Sarah Long." A souvenir of 'Playschool.' (Photo: BBC Television)

script, showed me the studio — after the labyrinth of corridors at the Television Centre this would be child's play — and I confirmed the same petrol arrangements applied.

"See you at half past one," Albert breezed, "ready for a two o'clock start. Lunch in the canteen any time you like."

We spent a cold but bright morning looking at Manchester's shops, to Dee's delight, and after lunch we unhitched the trailer and began manoeuvring the van into the studios, with two men guiding me because of the hazards of overhead lights and stacked scenery.

Rehearsals started at two amid a buzz of activity, and I was introduced to the new presenter, Stuart McGuggan, whom I'd seen in the comedy series *It Ain't Half Hot, Mum;* Sarah Long was also there, with a smile of remembrance for *Ceōl* and me. The lessons we'd learned in London still worked and, after just two runs through with an assistant, we had the fade-out problem licked. My lines were simple, but I was opening with *Teddybears' Picnic* and this time I started to rush my lines.

Stuart calmed me. "Take your time, take your time. Just relax." I was probably a little on edge because Dee was watching it all.

After a tea-break we had a full run-through and sorted out the final points, then I saw the lady producer walking across the studio and coming to see me. I had obviously done something wrong.

"Leonard, we heard you camped in the car park last night."

"True," I said. "So what?"

"It's not allowed, because of the IRA bomb scares." She smiled. "Don't worry; we'll find you another site for tonight."

"Not too far away," I begged. I wanted to be on the road early the next morning to avoid the rush-hour traffic in Manchester and in London.

The recording itself went quite well, but they had to do a few retakes, although not of my doing; Stuart fluffled his lines twice over the title of the *Teddybears' Picnic*. Finally, after six hours, we had put together a 25-minute programme! And then there was supper in the staff restaurant, so that it was around 10pm when a secretary came to me with the news that the only caravan site they could offer was at the Charnock motorway services. I smiled my thanks, but we were certainly not going to pitch there: if you can tolerate the slamming of doors and roar of engines, you still can't have a hot breakfast as the use of gas cylinders is prohibited. Curse the IRA!

It was late. The staff was already leaving and I guessed there would soon be only the security people left. As we went out to the car park, with the prospect of an hour's drive to a noisy motorway pull-off looking daunting, I wondered what would happen if we couldn't start the new engine . . . ?

Dee read my thoughts. "You can't . . ."

"We'll be away at first light; who'll know anything about it?" But I didn't bargain on a sharp frost, and when I tried to start the engine in the morning, it wouldn't. It was probably a combination of the new motor and the thickening of the oil, but fate had played me at my own game.

I decided not to risk running the battery flat, so we had breakfast, then I phoned the Automobile Association — and learned we may have to wait two hours, due to the many non-start calls that morning. I told them not to bother; I took out the heating plugs, warmed them on the gas ring, and the engine fired first time. It was 8.45 when we pulled away, still with no questions asked, and we were home before dusk, with the engine satisfactorily run-in.

The bigger engine was a boon and the Transit was much easier to handle, which was lucky as the television exposure increased the bookings, notably the midweek county shows. It was about this time in what I call my retirement, that Dee and her sister tactfully said that they were going back to more gainful occupation: they enrolled at the local hospital as part-time nurses. I think they must have felt redundant as there was no engine to fire and water, and only one vehicle was needed.

That reminded me of the words of old George Print, a fairground proprietor who had got rid of steam because, in his words, "they were slow, dirty and labour-intensive." He may have cut out the dirt and the overmanning, but he also lost a great deal of character and atmosphere: it was comparable with the shock that passengers on the *Venice-Simplon Orient Express* experience when they realise their luxury coaches are to be hauled by a diesel engine. George's sentiments were definitely not mine, and already I bitterly regretted having parted with *Prince*.

But I certainly was not slow and labour-intensive, although I was probably dirty at the end of the day. Just look at the appendix and study the bookings I was fulfilling — such as leaving Camborne, Cornwall, late on 20 August after attending the West of England

124

Rally, and being in the Aldeburgh Carnival in Suffolk the following day. That was perhaps an extreme example, but I was certainly pushing myself — I wouldn't have done it if I didn't enjoy it.

So with no steam engine, how did I generate electricity for the organ, you may well ask. As I explained earlier, all *Prince* had ever done was to provide air for the bellows, while the Land-Rover generated the electricity — until the price of diesel became prohibitive. These days, I always ensured there would be a 13-amp power point for me to plug into, or a traction engine to supply me with 110v DC. Using a universal system was indeed a blessing, and an organ hooked up to a full-scale traction engine appealed almost as much as one hooked up to a model such as *Prince*.

With the growing popularity of the fair organ, there came a demand to have a recording made; after all, people had been taping the music for several years. I asked Albert Barber, producer of *Playschool*, if he could advise me and on his recommendation I contacted a small company, Response Records. The recording engineer said I would need to have the organ indoors to cut out all unwanted sounds such as birdsong and the distant noise of traffic, as well as to avoid wind on the microphone.

The only suitable place I could find was an empty barn belonging to Phil Ives. He suggested a Sunday as being the quietest, so I met the recording engineer in Bedford and we made our way to the barn.

I was surprised at just how complicated a job it was to rig up the various microphones in exact spots, but after the hours spent in television studios I should have had an inkling. Once things were set up, we began recording. We had finished the two LPs and were on the smaller disc of carols when the telephone rang, immediately ruining the music we were currently taping. A telephone in a barn? After I told the caller that Phil was not at home, I left the receiver off the handset while we re-recorded the carols. The session was a success, but some years later I began to think I played the music a little too quickly.

The LPs were called *Leonard Brooks's Chiappa Fairground Organ*, and the first one offered on the first side:

The March Of The Gladiators
Post Horn Gallop
Sussex By The Sea

Lambeth Walk
The Teddy Bears' Picnic
The Skaters' Waltz.
The second side had:
I Do Like To Be Beside the Seaside
Chilli Bon Bon
Jack In The Box
The Fairground March
It's A Long Way To Tipperary
Petite Valse
The second disc featured modern music as well as traditional. On the first side were:
A medley, *Tie A Yellow Ribbon Round The Old Oak Tree* and *Alexander's Ragtime Band*
King Cotton
How're You Gonna Keep 'Em Down On The Farm
Another medley, *Tea For Two* and *Ma, He's Making Eyes At Me*
Whispering
The other side had:
Over The Waves
Row, Row, Row
Waiting For The Robert E. Lee
Middy March
Barcelona
Y Viva España
And for Christmas carols we had: *Once In Royal David's City; Good King Wenceslas; God Rest Ye Merry, Gentlemen; Oh, Come All Ye Faithful; While Shepherds Watched* and *Jingle Bells.*

Albert Barber designed the sleeves, using the photo he had taken of *Ceōl* at my home, and the blurb on the back gave a brief history of the organ: "(it) is the most-travelled in preservation. It has helped rally promoters, Lions clubs, Rotary clubs, Round Table and other charity organisations, to collect many thousands of pounds. It has appeared many times on television, both BBC and Independent channels, radio and in newsreels. Perhaps the appearances on BBC Television's Children's Programme, *Playschool*, were the most popular. Children always remember it, everywhere it goes, with "Look, mum — *Playschool*'"

Was there no end to *Ceōl*'s fame?

13: ONE OF THOSE DAYS

LIFE ON THE road has its ups and downs, particularly when you're travelling alone. After the recording session I headed on to the West Midlands Show, a classic county event at Shrewsbury that I was to attend until 1985. I always pitched on the public green beside a gypsy fortune-teller, but I remember this particular show for the RAF exhibit, a huge vehicle with a wartime barrage balloon tethered to it.

Incredible though it may seem, some local youngsters came around during the night and managed to release the balloon, which drifted away towards Wales trailing its steel hawser. Next day the show was rife with the rumour that the gasbag had to be shot down as its trailing cable was a menace to overhead electricity cables, but I suspect the 'blimp' went up and up until the rarefied atmosphere burst it.

I was very much down to earth when I took *Ceōl* to a Saturday event at Beckenham, in south London. So many things went wrong on this trip that I wrote an article about them in *Keyframe*. After the usual checks — oil, petrol (this was before the van had had its motor changed), tyres, radiator, brakes and lights; and in the caravan, food, gas and water — I left home around noon on Friday, expecting to arrive around three o'clock.

I had travelled for no more than half an hour when steam started hissing from around the bonnet. Oh, God — trouble! But when I opened the bonnet I saw it was only a missing radiator cap. I looked back along the road but, of course, couldn't see it, so I topped up from the spare can (as breakdown teams sold water at up to £30 a gallon on motorways, I always carried some), made a temporary plug from some rags, and drove slowly for the next few miles until I found a service station that stocked rad caps. A minor delay, but it had set me back an hour.

By two I was approaching the Blackwall Tunnel; it was a hot day and a traffic hold-up in the tunnel could cause some engines to overheat. No problems. But the long, hard slog up the hill to Blackheath made the engine heat up and at the top I pulled off onto a loop road to let things cool and take a little refreshment.

As the motor was so hot I opened the bonnet and caught the unmistakable whiff of petrol. Now, I had recently bought a newfangled locking petrol tank cap with, as the salesman had proudly told me, a pressure seal to prevent loss by evaporation.

The trouble was, the seal had caused pressure to build up in the fuel system so much that the petrol was squirting out of a small crack in the flexible pipe, dangerously near the overheated exhaust manifold. I needed somebody to unlock the cap and release that pressure, but there were no pedestrians near this deserted loop road and I leaned over the hot engine with my thumb on the hole for what seemed to be a long time. It was a horrifying thought that the whole lot could have gone up in flames in the Blackwall Tunnell, taking Ceòl with it.

After a while an old man ambled along the path, and I called him over. "I'm in trouble here — can you help me?"

He looked perplexed: I wondered if he were deaf. That would be just my luck. I shouted: "Can you get my keys, please? They're in the ignition switch."

He took his time finding the keys and bringing them to me. With my free hand I located the one that unlocked the pressure cap, then I had to tell him where to go and what to do. Eventually he managed to release the cap because when I carefully took my thumb off the fracture, the petrol had stopped flooding. I went around the van to thank the old fellow, but he had already ambled fifty yards down the road.

My concern was now with the pipe. When I examined it in detail it began crumbling in my hand. So now what? The AA would take at least two hours to get here on a Friday afternoon. Away in the distance I could see a service station but, twenty minutes later when I reached it on foot, I found it sold nothing but petrol and ice-cold drinks.

I hurried back to the van, my brain looking for any way out of trouble, when I remembered there may be a piece of copper tubing in the 'junk box.' Glory be! It was still there! I took another half hour to make a temporary but serviceable repair then cautiously drove on, with the rag that had earlier plugged the radiator now stuffed in the filler pipe in place of the pressure cap: I would get a tiny hole drilled in it before using it again.

My service manual told me there was a Ford agency in a back street in Catford, so I turned off the main road and navigated my way, half my attention on the map and the other half on the caravan I was towing. I pulled up a hundred yards from the agency and bought a new flexible hose, but my repair looked so good I decided to fit the replacement later: I was running quite late.

The Friday evening traffic was building up as I wended my way back towards the main road, at one point having to bump the caravan over the kerb on a tight corner. I suppose you can guess what happened: within a quarter of a mile that tyre had a puncture. It just wasn't my day!

There was nowhere to park the Transit and the caravan, so I had to unhitch and manhandle the trailer into one gap — no easy task with a soft tyre — then leave the Transit further up the street. And that operation set me back another hour. How I wished Dee was with me to give me moral support — and to make me a cup of tea and sandwiches!

At long last, tired, hungry and dirty, and with the setting sun making driving difficult, I pulled into the showground. My planned three o'clock arrival was five hours overdue. After a meal and a wash, I met an old friend in the bar and over a cold beer told him of my hectic journey.

"You know why, don't you?" he said. "It's Friday the thirteenth!"

Then why didn't *he* have three breakdowns as well? But I thought it better not to ask him. If it was any consolation, Saturday the fourteenth was no better: it rained all day — and my friend got just as wet as I did.

THAT WAS MY worst day for mechanical problems, and I was expecting more trouble on each journey I made for several weeks, but I did the Suffolk Show, the Essex Show, a trip to Devon, and to John Carter's Windsor Forest Steam Rally with no problems.

Indeed, it was an ice cream vendor who had the problems at Windsor. John told him the rally had its full quota of ice cream vans, and that he would have to go. The obstinate vendor said he was there, and he was going to operate come what may, but I don't think he expected two of John's strong-arm men to put in an appearance. They asked him politely but when he refused again they started to rock the van so alarmingly that he got the message at once. He went.

John's lads patrolled the perimeter to deter the efforts of people who sought entry by means other than the pay booths. John also had the answer to the pass-out system: he had a rubber stamp and printed your pass-out on your hand as you left; you showed your hand as you came back in. This is the system that the Walt Disney company uses at its theme parks, and I'd really like to know if Walt borrowed the idea from John?

After Windsor came a visit to North Weald Aerodrome, and then to what might appear to be the most ridiculous booking I ever had — the Cambridge Museum of Technology, housed in a sewage pumping station museum near the city. In truth, the station had ceased to operate and its old machinery had been preserved as a self-contained museum, with other equipment added, including two Hathorn Davey steam pumps. Later, Fred Dibnah, the steeplejack who made his reputation on television, rebuilt the chimney.

Then I went to Southend-on-Sea for a street collection, to a fête at Ashford, to rallies at Knowl Hill and Reading, with the Aldeburgh Carnival in Suffolk the next day, then Stoneleigh Rally and on to the Bun Feast in Bungay on 4 August. Life was busy!

There's no connection between a bun and the town's name, but it's a nice idea. This little Suffolk community which now specialises in printing was a major power in the 12th century, and Hugh Bigod, the first Earl of Norfolk, built a castle here, its walls 18 feet thick at the base and soon to reach 90 feet high (5.5m by 27m). The fortress scared Henry II so much that he ordered it to be destroyed, but substantial ruins still stand in the town centre to this day.

Fire destroyed the timber-and-thatch town in 1688, but Bungay has kept the charm of its rebuilt 17th-century houses and is a delightful place to visit. The Bun Show was a Saturday-only event and I slept in my caravan in the field, as I had to get up early to be in Harefield, Middlesex, for a Sunday afternoon recital.

THIS WAS TO BE another of 'those days.' By late morning I was on the North Circular Road, the A406, a dreadful road at the best of times in those days before the M25 was opened.

130

Catch the North Circular at the wrong time and it seemed to be filled with crawling milk floats, commuters racing to work, or heavy lorries. Today, a Sunday, it was easy . . . until I glanced at my speedometer and saw a red light glowing.

I dismissed it: the generator had stopped charging, I told myself. I probably needed new carbon brushes and in the meantime I was not charging the battery; no problem until it came to night driving. But as I approached Staples Corner, where the IRA was later to explode its bombs, I heard an ominous rattle from the engine and I stopped at once. The red glow wasn't for the generator — it was the oil warning light.

I coasted down the slope ahead, and used the engine as little as possible until I could pull off onto a factory forecourt. The watchman saw me arrive and as soon as he knew I was carrying a vintage organ he was sympathetic and ready to help. He let me use the works phone to call the AA, as it was obvious this time that I wasn't going to make it under my own power. I lifted the bonnet and propped it up with a piece of wooden dowelling as I put oil into the motor. The dowelling was still in place when the AA man arrived; he tried the engine, listened, and said it was a tow-in job; he guessed I'd damaged the bearings, but he rang his office and called his inspector out.

While the inspector had his head under the bonnet, my old pal Goff Ratcliffe was driving past and, recognising my outfit, stopped to offer his help. Of course, there was not enough room for two heads peering into the engine and Goff accidentally knocked the dowelling away as he came out, bringing the bonnet crashing down on the AA inspector.

The poor fellow didn't see the funny side of it, but the original AA man and I found it difficult to keep a straight face.

"I wish bloody bystanders wouldn't interfere!" the inspector cursed — but Goff had gone.

The inspector tried the engine but confirmed it as a tow-in job, and called the breakdown truck; *its* driver looked at the Transit, its load, and the caravan, and decided his tow rope wasn't strong enough. "No matter," I told him. "I've got a high-tensile chain for emergencies."

We snapped a shackle during the tow when the breakdown truck stopped, let slack into the chain, then started off too quickly, but before dusk we were home with no further damage done.

No, I didn't make it to the recital, but that was one of only two occasions when I failed to turn up for a booking.

Five days later, with a rebuilt engine, I took *Ceōl* to the Windmill Fête at Rayleigh, and I noticed the mechanics had put labels saying OIL and GEN on the red warning lights.

Leonard and Richard Allen (left) of Allen Motors, Romford, show off one of 'Ceōl' s music cards. (Photo: Ford Motor Co)

14: VISITORS, WELCOME AND UNWELCOME

I MADE A SERIES of shorter journeys to run-in the new bearings, and when I had to use the caravan I begged Dee's help to tow it with the Land-Rover.

And that's how we went to Henham Park. Henham, not to be confused with a village in Essex, is one of the strangest places I went to. The present owner, the Earl of Stradbroke, was an Australian sheep farmer when he inherited the title unexpectedly, and he scandalised the locality by living in an utterly bizarre manner, totally out of keeping with accepted aristocratic ideas; at one time he wanted to start a nudist colony there, but the public outcry put a stop to it. He had 14 or so children, most of whom were named from local villages — Wangford Rous, Heydon Rous, Blyford Rous and, I wouldn't be surprised to learn, a Walberswick Rous. He also caused a stir by selling the family jewels to raise the cash to keep the estate going, just how he wanted it.

I must give the earl his due; he eventually became a respected and admired part of the community, and Henham was one of my favourite rallies, managed by my friend Len Murray until his death in 1986, but the rally itself kept running until 1994 when it moved to Yoxford, just down the road. Was there a Yoxford Rous, I wonder?

Henham Rally was noted for — among other features — three buxom wenches who specialised in dancing the can-can. I put a suitable book into the organ and every hour, on the hour, the ladies danced, kicking their legs high and showing their frillies. It was a popular event with the menfolk, some of whom were very elderly indeed; I used to notice that they arrived early in order to get the best viewpoint! Don't ask me what Dee thought of it.

During one particular Henham Rally I was playing *Ceōl's* music into John Carter's newly-acquired roundabout, which didn't yet have its own working organ. Within minutes we noticed that the crowd had swelled a great deal and the roundabout was riding to capacity. I came down from the Transit and realised that the church in nearby Wangford village had a service going out on the public address system: don't ask me the why about that, either, but it was a happy event, like a marriage or a baptism. But the poor vicar was rapidly losing his congregation to the rival attractions of the fairground.

I called to John and, poker-faced, asked: "Do you think we ought to stop while the vicar is on the PA?"

"Len, you've got to be kidding! Stop now? Not bloody likely!"

On another occasion at Henham, a man asked me to take *Ceōl* to a fête at Woodton in Norfolk. "You must come. It's a lovely show and our chairman is the local MP, James Prior. You've heard of him?"

"Of course I have." Mr Prior was the current Secretary of State for Northern Ireland. "But I bet he won't be there," I added.

"I promise you he will."

I took *Ceōl* to the fête at a later date and forgot about the famous chairman until late in the afternoon when the organiser came along with Mr Prior. "See? I told you he'd be here. I've brought him along to meet you."

I talked with the Secretary of State for Northern Ireland for quite a while without once mentioning politics or, I hope, interrupting affairs of state.

In our spare time we found Henham was the ideal base to see something of the surrounding countryside, and I often went to the nearby towns of Beccles, Halesworth and Southwold to play a few tunes in the street and draw attention to the rally.

Over the years, *Ceōl* became very popular in this part of the country, probably because East Anglia had a strong tradition of travelling fairs going back for centuries, and those at Wisbech, King's Lynn, Norwich and Southwold managed to survive the longest. I remember that Norwich was a great city for charity events, although on looking through my records I found I played there only in 1979 and 1981. In fact, one of my longest bookings was at Lowestoft when I played *Ceōl* every evening for a week in February 1979 to mark the opening of the *Seagull Theatre*, converted from a disused school. It was cold!

Also in 1981 I was invited back to Southwold in early December as an honoured visitor to attend the mayoral switching-on of the town's Christmas lights, and in 1984, towards the end of my time on the road, I gave a carol recital at Halesworth.

The gatecrashers — or maybe I should say 'hedgehoppers' — at Henham were no problem, but at other events they became a major headache. That was the case at a big event, including a full-fledged fair, in a park at Ipswich. Late in the afternoon I had cause to visit the control office where I heard that some man had mingled with the official collectors at the entrance and during the day had taken a sizeable amount of money from motorists.

A similar thing happened at a steam rally. The car park was free, and the visitors then walked to a pay booth at the entrance to the ground. Two astute crooks had cut a gap in the hedge and made a shorter way into the rally field, and were charging their own entrance fee.

One of the most unusual visitors came to me at a steam rally in Holton, on the eastern edge of Oxford in 1978. He invited me to a college end-of-term party at the village of Cuddesdon two miles to the south, and five days later at the end of June. I had an engagement in the meantime at a hospital fête in Essex, but as I was due back in Andover for a rally the day after the party, I accepted.

I was back at Cuddesdon in the late afternoon and started playing at 6pm, then the gentleman who had invited me asked if I had *Macnamara's Band* in *Ceōl*'s repertoire.

"I certainly have. I'll play it next."

"Good. Would you like a drink?"

"I wouldn't mind a pale sherry."

He was back a few minutes later with the drink, then he said in an aside: "Any time you see me coming with my — ah, friend — I would like you to play *Macnamara's Band*. Can do?"

"Can do," I agreed.

"And go into the hall any time you want and help yourself to the food and drink. Right?"

"Right."

I saw him several times that evening with his 'friend' and each time I switched to *Macnamara's Band*. And each time he brought me another sherry. It was an enjoyable evening and I went back for six years, but not all of them are recorded in my diary.

One of my long journeys was undoubtedly to the Wales and West

Show held at David Broome's stud farm at Newport, Gwent, where I played for three enjoyable days. David himself was away at an event, but I met his father, who organised this show, which was no mean feat.

Two months later I was back in the West Country at a publicity recital at St Ives for the local Round Table. I drove into the town with no problem, despite the awkward one-way system, and I played on the jetty all day long in glorious sunshine. But when it was time to go I was given my directions: "Left, left again — and mind the hill." Hill! We have nothing like it in Essex, and I think it was worse than the gradient at Stonehaven. I put the Transit in bottom gear and just managed to crawl to the top: if I'd had the caravan on tow there would have been no way I could have made it.

I moved on a few miles to St Agnes for the West of England Rally which fitted nicely into the next two days. This was a great event, packed with a wide range of exhibits — one of which was my former steam traction engine, *Firefly*. Dear old *Firefly*! Seeing her again brought back many memories, as well as a touch of nostalgia for departed *Prince*. And among the visitors I met were Mr Warren and George Hawkins, both of whom had owned *Firefly* before me. George gave me the glad news that although the engine had had other owners after me, he had bought her again, and I was pleased to note the leviathan was in better shape than when I had first seen her.

What struck me particularly was that in a very hilly county there was sufficient reasonably flat land to hold a steam rally. I saw a little of St Agnes, notably the 'Stippy-Stappy', a row of miners' cottages built on a very steep hill.

Sadly, there was no opportunity to see anything of nearby Camborne, but I heard plenty of its history. A century ago the area was the world's leading copper producer and in 1856 more than 200,000 tons of copper ore were dug. An early mine collapsed many years ago leaving a hole 100 yards across at the top and looking like one of those saucers created in Nevada, USA, after a nuclear bomb has been exploded underground. John Wesley is said to have preached in the bottom of the saucer in 1762.

I suppose the Cornish visit must go down in my records as the starting point for the longest drive I ever did with *Ceōl* as I had to be at Aldeburgh in Suffolk the next morning for the Carnival.

I usually went to the Royal Showground at Stoneleigh, south of Coventry, for the August Bank Holiday Monday, and often moved to the Leicester Show in the city's Abbey Park as the Tuesday was a local holiday. One of my visitors at Abbey Park was Tommy Wadsworth of Radio Leicester who found the organ music so fascinating that he asked if he could use some of it as his signature tune on his programme. I was flattered and pleased to agree.

But the Salvation Army stand near me in the park had had a most unwelcome visitor. The husband and wife team from Leicester had worked hard for two days, doing a lot of fundraising. As we we packing up to go home I noticed they were distressed; somebody had waited until the collection box was at its fullest, and had then stolen it. It's a low type of person who could steal from the Sally Ann and I felt almost as badly about it as the couple did, but I kept a cheerful face.

"Don't worry," I said. "I can easily make that amount in one day with Ceōl. Tell you what: I do a Christmas collection in Bedford. I'll go over to Leicester the next day and you can have the entire collection." And that is what I eventually did.

My most unforgettable visitor introduced herself by phoning me one evening to tell me about her charity called Children's World, and to ask if we could come to her big two-day summer event in Glastonbury. It was a long way from Essex and I said I would think about it and call her back; casually I asked her name.

"Arabella Churchill."

"I can't forget a name like that," I said, "but I bet you're no relation."

"You'd lose your money, I'm afraid. I'm the grand-daughter of Sir Winston."

Now, as for so many people of my age, Winston Churchill was a national hero, and I told Arabella we would be there whatever happened. We arrived early in the day straight from the previous rally at Knowl Hill, near Maidenhead, and camped in a delightful caravan site just outside Glastonbury. I phoned Miss Churchill and she sent one of the helpers to see us, then while we were talking to him we had the idea of going into Street to make a collection a day early; there was a good site available.

Just in case you wonder about the legality of collecting money on the public highway, I'd better explain that one needs permission from the local council *and* from the police, and it is usually a legal requirement to announce in the local paper the amount collected. Every collection I made fulfilled these rules, but I never got involved with the regulations — the organisers always did it.

I knew we had raised a phenomenal £99,850, plus or minus a pound or so, since we started, and we needed just £150 to take our total into six figures. But I also knew Fridays are not the best days for collecting, and we started slowly. Street has only one main street, if you'll pardon the expression, and it wasn't a pedestrian precinct where collectors can work easily, but the organisers plodded on steadily while I played the music and drew the crowds.

Towards midday a lady approached us, and I knew at once that it had to be Arabella Churchill. We both smiled. "You recognised the chin?" she asked, and I had to agree. When I pointed out that we needed more collectors, she sent two circus clowns from the show, and their antics soon had the locals laughing and putting money in the tins. That evening I knew the six-digit figure had been passed.

JOHN CARTER'S VISITOR problem was with a guest who didn't arrive. This was at John's Air Show at Bookham, and when I saw him early on the Sunday afternoon he was distraught. "That bloody Red Baron hasn't turned up."

"What Red Baron would that be?"

"The guy who pretends he's the First World War German Air Ace, of course. He's due to fight the Royal Flying Corps, but how can we have a dogfight with only one plane?"

"Can't you borrow one?"

"Oh, yes? Do you happen to have a vintage triplane in the back of your van?"

The Red Baron never arrived, and the dogfight was cancelled. I found out why the next day when I saw a report in the newspaper. *Ex-Luftwaffe Fighter Pilot Killed in Air Display.* The Red Baron had been performing in France when his plane crashed, killing him instantly.

I had had a strange visitor myself during the air show. A tall, bearded man wandered up to the organ and began talking to me. We spoke for several minutes before he continued on his way, but a moment later someone else hurried to me to ask what the bearded

138

man had said to me.

"General conversation," I answered. "Why?"

"You know who that was, don't you?"

I shook my head. "No idea. Should I?"

"That was Prince Michael, Duke of Kent!"

IN AUGUST 1979 I was also the visitor in for a surprise. The location was to be the Tower of London, one of the prime tourist attractions of the country, at one of the busiest weekends of the year, and the charity chosen for the collection was the Arthritis and Rheumatism Council. All the collectors thought we'd do well and I expected that, given the right conditions, *Ceōl* on her own would raise £1,000. On the day the weather was perfect, the publicity had been first-class, and there were plenty of tourists — but the money just didn't flow in. I put it down to the fact that most overseas visitors (except the Dutch, who regularly have fair organs in the streets of Amsterdam and the Hague) didn't understand the idea of charity collectons; as somebody said, "They probably think this is another London rip-off." *Ceōl* and I worked very hard for our £200, and I never went to the Tower again.

The very next day I headed north to the Rutland County Show, although the county itself, England's smallest, had been swallowed by Leicestershire five years earlier. It was a first-rate event and the folk really liked *Ceōl*'s music, yet it was to be my one and only visit.

A few days later I paid my first visit to Brands Hatch, the Kentish motor racing circuit, but this particular crowd had come to see machines powered by steam, not petrol. No hundred-miles-an-hour laps with screaming engines and roaring exhausts; instead, just the puff-puff of steam, and speeds no more than running pace. It must have been the most peaceful day that Brands Hatch had ever had; no wonder the event became a permanent fixture.

Towards the end of the 1978 season when I was busy with the pre-Chistmas charity collections, I arranged to spend two days in Bedford Town Centre as the *Playschool* team had again expressed an interest in filming me — this time in the street, raising money for charity.

The filming was to be on a Friday in Church Square. I arrived extra early, parked on the pavement in my usual spot, then went off for a hot coffee. When I came back I found a policeman standing by the van.

"Good morning, sir. Is this your vehicle?"

"Yes."

"Then you are Leonard Brooks and you come from Harold Wood?"

I smiled. "Ah! I see you go to the rallies."

"Not so, sir." He didn't explain any further but I realised he was just showing off the newly-computerised vehicle registration system and his personal radio-phone. From now on the police could wave down a vehicle and have its owner's name and address fed to them by computer and radio before the driver could step out of his cab. But this policeman had other ideas.

"Why are you parked on the pavement, sir?"

"There's a fairground organ in the van. The BBC is going to make a programme about it this morning. We've got permission to park on the pavement."

He softened a little, so the devil in me added: "Why not stick around? You might get on the telly!"

At that moment the organiser appeared with the relevant paperwork. The policeman satisfied himself that I was telling the truth, and he became quite friendly. I don't know if he stuck around, but I didn't see him on screen.

Soon the television people arrived with all the paraphernalia that goes with making an outside recording. There were trucks, extra large floodlights, women in hard hats, and lots of microphones. Soon a huge crowd had gathered and if the policeman was around he would have been busy in traffic control. We managed to get some sort of normality in front of the cameras, and I began playing Christmas carols. Even when the television crews had packed up and gone, the crowds still milled around, and Bedford Round Table had one of its biggest collections that day.

Collections already accounted for more of my bookings than any other event, particularly at the colder times of the year, and as the seventies gave way to the eighties I was at my busiest. According to my diary, I attended 62 events in 1977, 71 the next year, and my record of 77 bookings in 1979, keeping me occupied on site for 96 days, not including all the travelling time. The following year the total dropped by one, and by 1981 it was down to 61 as *anno domini* began to catch up on me. In my last year I kept only 22 engagements over 24 days, 16 of the events being in Essex and with Lowestoft my furthest from home. And nine of those bookings were purely for street collections although I gathered money on several other events.

Let me tell you about the South of England Show where I met a Mr Elias who told me about the hospital school at Lingfield, Surrey, with which he was involved. I found I could sympathise with the work the school did for disabled children, and I accepted his invitation to go to the fête, held in June. It was a big event, and that year's celebrity visitor was the comedian and musician Roy Castle. In the end, I agreed to spend the week before the big day in that area, playing *Ceōl* in the surrounding towns of Oxted, Edenbridge, East Grinstead, Caterham and Reigate — but I haven't entered all those places in my diary.

Some of the nurses from the school joined me each day and not only did we collect a considerable sum, we also created interest in the fête. The fête itself was a new concept for me: the parking was free and there was no charge for admission — no wonder it attracted tremendous crowds.

I went there for the next six years as I thought it was one of the most worthy causes I could support; in my later years I was also attending the steam rally at the nearby Lingfield Racecourse.

I almost forgot my casual meeting with boxing and snooker promoter Barry Hearn at a little fête near his home in Standon Massey, Essex. Snooker star Steve Davis was at the event, and impressed me with his ability to make friends with the children.

In all my years on the road, my most prestigious visitor would have been the Queen Mother, as I was invited to County Hall, Westminster, to entertain the guests at the great lady's eightieth birthday. *Ceōl* was playing on the terrace, diagonally opposite the Houses of Parliament, and I had an excellent view of the Queen Mother as she passed downriver aboard the Royal Barge. But I never got any closer than that.

I had a very pleasant visitor shortly after I arrived in Bristol to play at the 'Kids' Show,' a fairly comprehensive event in the new docks complex, where exhibition buildings have replaced the historic quays. I reported to the show manager for the necessary details. Yes, he had booked me into a caravan site; yes, the show would start on Friday — this was only Monday, as I had come from

Glastonbury and decided to have a few days in the city instead of facing the long haul home and back again.

As I was talking to him a young lady from Radio West came into the office and I found myself telling her about *Ceōl*. The show manager said: "Why don't you give her a tune, Len?"

She nodded. "Yes. Why not? I can record it right away."

"Hold on. I'll be with you in five minutes." I led them to the Transit van and opened its side, and plugged the cable into one of the many sockets in the building. I switched on the full lights, although it was broad daylight, but it added to the atmosphere. Then I put *The Teddybears' Picnic* on to play.

The radio journalist was ready for the occasion. She faded in the music then spoke into her microphone: "And here is the lovely organ. You can hear it playing *The Teddybears' Picnic* just as it did on television. And there are little ladies on the front of the organ, beating time and striking bells. It's a mass of colour and light; you must come and see it." She switched off and smiled. "That'll help draw the crowds."

I did my own little bit to draw the crowds in the three spare days I had, by playing *Ceōl* in the street — but not too much to spoil the novelty.

Bristol! I also took time off to see something of the city where Sebastian Cabot was born, and from where he and his father set sail in 1497 with a crew of 18 to reach Newfoundland, only five years after Columbus had discovered North America for the Europeans.

From 1552 Bristol began trading in high-value merchandise such as tobacco and cacao from the Americas, which ultimately gave rise to the city's major manufacturers, such as W.D. and H.O. Wills, the tobacco giants, and Frys the Quaker chocolate makers. The docks also saw wool exported and Portuguese wine and African slaves imported. And then, of course, in 1838 Isambard Brunel launched his first steamship, the *Great Western*, here. And while I was in the city his other ship, the *Great Britain* was being restored after spending years aground on a reef in the Falkland Islands.

Ah, Bristol! The 'Kids' Show' was so successful that I was invited back, this time to a fishing tackle exhibition. But I never made it.

15: FIRE AND WATER

ONE OF THE most horrifying moments of my life happened on the North Circular Road, the A406. The highway belies its name; it's not a circular route at all, but a hotch-potch of mainly suburban roads put together to make a passage around the north of London in the days before the building of the M25, the world's longest orbital motorway.

It was on a hot Friday that Dee, Irene and I set out shortly after midday for a John Carter event in Berkshire. We had left the Land-Rover at home so all three of us were squeezed into the Transit's cab, which wasn't too comfortable.

We were delayed by road-widening work on the Finchley part of the North Circular and, because of the caravan on tow, I had kept to the nearside lane, for which I am eternally grateful.

The engine stalled. I tried to start it, but it didn't fire. I tried again — and this time it fired with a vengeance: flames shot out from under the bonnet. The womenfolk scrambled from the cab and, as soon as I could switch off and put the handbrake on, I followed.

By the time we were all on the pavement the engine seemed well alight. I took a step towards it, trying to help but not knowing what to do.

Dee screamed: "Come away from it, Len! It'll explode!"

Explode? Was this to be the end of *Ceōl*, incinerated in a traffic jam? Was this where my travels would come to an abrupt finish, in the ignominy of a fire?

The traffic was moving again, but it kept moving. Nobody stopped to help. Nobody cared.

Then I thought of the caravan. Should I unhitch it and try to save it? Would the pressure of traffic allow it?

The caravan! Suddenly I remembered it had a fire extinguisher aboard! I fumbled with keys, threw open the door and snatched the red cylinder, not bothering to check whether it was filled with water, foam or powder, but I did briefly wonder whether it would work: it was there when we bought the caravan.

I rushed to the front of the Transit, ignoring Dee's screams for me to come away. There was no way I could open the bonnet so I sprayed the contents of the extinguisher through the grille. Within seconds a dense cloud of white vapour enveloped us, but the flames were suffocated. The fire was out.

I took our five-gallon water canister from the back of the van and doused the bonnet until it stopped hissing. Then, cautiously, I opened up the engine and poured more water over the smouldering electrics and battery. The emergency was over, and we were stuck.

The womenfolk were obviously relieved. "What now?" Dee asked.

I took stock of our location, causing a traffic bottleneck at the approach to major road works, and outside a big cemetery, an ominous hint of what might have happened to us.

"What now? I'll call the AA." There was nothing else I could do. I went into the cemetery to see if there was an office with a phone, but retraced my steps without any luck. However, Dee and Irene were talking to an angel: in truth, a woman who lived on the other side of the busy road.

"I saw what happened," she explained. "It was terrible, wasn't it? But you was so lucky. It's a terrible road, this, and nobody stops to help nobody. And with the caravan an' all. And your wife says you've got an organ inside. I love organs. I really love organs, an' traction engines. But I came over to see if you want to use my phone. I mean, so many phones in London is vandalised these days. Terrible, what things is coming to."

Leaving the ladies in charge, I followed the talkative angel to a footbridge over the busy road, which explained why she hadn't come ministering to us earlier. The AA promised to be with us soon so I took my leave of our saviour and made the long walk back across the road. By then the foreman on the road widening job, a genial Irishman, had forced his way through the traffic to offer us a section of coned-off highway for the Transit and the caravan; he even held up the cars while his men helped push our convoy into this spot of relative safety.

In gratitude I told him *Ceól* had spent her working life in Ireland, and I gave him a postcard showing the organ.

144

The AA breakdown driver said he couldn't tow the Transit and the caravan back to Harold Wood, but he'd get us to a Ford service depot in Finchley. I was so relieved to know that *Ceōl* was safe that I would have agreed to almost anything. As soon as we reached the depot I called one of our daughters and asked her to come and collect three weary, shocked travellers. Then, while we waited we inspected the damage. It was extensive and would mean the replacement of everything but the engine and radiator: all the wiring, ignition switch, battery, distributor, fan belt, hoses, and paintwork.

Twelve days later I went back to Finchley and collected the convoy. The lesson I had learned from that incident was that one should always carry a fire extinguisher, *instantly available*. To prove I had learned my lesson, I bought two.

How it was done: 'Prince' powering 'Ceōl''s bellows. (Photo: Cheryl Brooks)

AFTER THE GREAT FIRE came an influx of new places to explore, most of them beside the sea or with other links with water. There was the first of several visits to Clacton-on-Sea, with a summer fête at the now-closed Passmore Edwards rehabilitation home, and the staff collected with *Ceōl* in the town centre before the show. I took the caravan there for a five-day stay and parked it so I could wake up and see the sea.

Clacton had a reputation of being a little bit kiss-me-quick and candyfloss, doubtless due to the visitors at Billy Butlin's holiday camp, but years later I was astounded to learn that Butlin had built on a site of worldwide archaeological importance. Scientists claim that what was then the oldest known man-made object, a fire-hardened wooden spear probably 300,000 years old, was found there in 1911. And they've found plenty of prehistoric elephant bones in the golf course.

Then there was the Romney, Hythe and Dymchurch Light Railway, started in 1927 by Jack Howey, a famous motor racer in his time. For a while the railway claimed to have the narrowest gauge of any public line in the world — 15 inches — but the latest claimant is the Wells and Walsingham Railway in Norfolk which has a 10.25 inch gauge. The RHDLR had nine steam locos when I started attending the annual rally for steam traction engines; on the first year I arrived several days early to advertise the event in Folkestone and Hythe.

Rochester's Dickens Week was a nice historial event, cashing in on the town's strong links with Charles Dickens. Dickens, and his character Pickwick, stayed at Eastgate House, High Street (Dickens called it Westgate House); *Great Expectations* was set on the marshes nearby and Miss Havisham's house is based on a property on Maidstone Road. Uncle Pumblechook lived on the High Street; the town has links with *Christmas Stories, Edwin Drood*, and was disguised in *Uncommercial Traveller* and *Mudfog Papers*.

I played *Ceōl* in the ruins of the castle, built in the reign of Henry I, and in the streets, while the townspeople took Dickens to their heart, many of them going about their daily life dressed in mid-nineteenth-century clothes, the women in crinolines and bonnets, the men in top hats, and small boys dressed as chimney sweeps. It was a pity that my only attendance at the Dickens Week was reduced to two days as I had come direct from the Sellindge Rally.

I found Leigh-on-Sea Regatta to be another interesting weekend event, and as I write I know that *Ceōl* still attends.

DESPITE THE REWIRING on the engine after the fire, the replacement diesel motor itself was now beginning to show distinct signs of fatigue; it was far from new when I had it and one day I drove carefully in order to see the row of digits change from a string of nines to one of zeros. I had raised one hundred thousand pounds for charity, and now the odometer stood at one hundred thousand miles, although God alone knew my actual mileage.

I mentioned it to a reporter at a rally and he suggested I contact the Ford Motor Company for help. As Ford already knew about the Transit, and *Ceōl*, I took his advice. The van was always fully laden with the organ, plus spares, the water drum, up to three people in the cab, and frequently a caravan on tow. And it had to face some extremely steep hills now and again. The engine certainly did some hard work — thinking back on it, I wondered how the original petrol motor had managed to cope with some of the demands I had made on it. The van itself must have been the best Transit to come from the Ford factory, as it had an E registration, first time around, making it a 1966 model.

The Ford Company did indeed help me, through a local dealer, and it was a wonderful sensation to know there was a *new* engine under that bonnet. To help run it in properly I did some short-journey events, but drove carefully on the one long-distance engagement, another of those West Country end-of-term parties, this one at Newton Abbot.

My greatest thrill was to be invited to the Open Day at the Temple Mills Railway Works at Stratford, east London, a place I had wanted to visit since my youth when it was part of the Great Eastern Railway network. In days gone by they used to work on the giant steam locomotives of every boy's dream, but even now there's still a lot of heavy engineering going on. Open days are rare, and I had an enjoyable time — and I like to think *Ceōl* helped make the day enjoyable for the visitors.

I went to the Dagenham Town Show the next day, then a few days later to the Kent County Show at Detling, near Maidstone, which completed the running-in of the motor. The Kent Show was always a favourite as it consistently had a good display of traction engines and old-time farm machinery: furthermore, the site was flat and the organisation excellent.

But there were problems ahead. Soon after having the new motor fitted, I had to acknowledge to myself that my days on the road were numbered. Although I was to continue until Christmas 1986, it was on a downhill path, the tempo of my decline gradually accelerating month by month. There would be no more journeys to the West Country and all too soon my activities would be confined to the south-east — Essex, London and Kent — with only rare engagements outside that area.

Unwillingly, I was having to face up to my second retirement.

Leonard Brooks raised the money, but Sacha Distel presented the cheque for research into muscular dystrophy. This was at the Truelove Children's Home, Ingatestone, Essex. (Photo: Peter Elgar, Brentwood)

16: JOURNEY'S END

BY THE SUMMER of 1983 my sight was deteriorating noticeably. It was most obvious when I was driving at night, as the vast grey areas lost their detail and I was looking at a world increasingly made up of bright lights and blackness. But I determined I would see the year out: I had 48 bookings from March to December.

I coped with the summer events, when the nights are short: favourites such as the Kent Show, Knowl Hill, the Aussie aristocrat at Henham Hall, and Hadlow Down. On the first of October I was back at St Bartholomew's Hospital in London for another street fair in Smithfield, similar to the one I had attended ten years earlier with *Prince*. I was amazed to find several people who remembered the miniature steam engine and asked about her. "Too expensive to run," I told them. The same would soon be true of me, if I had to ask Dee to do all the driving.

At the end of the year I had another eye test, with a follow-up in the spring. The report was gloomy and I had to face up to the reality that this would be my last full year as owner of *Ceōl*. I wouldn't keep her in a museum and if I couldn't take her out to meet the people, I would have to part with her.

It was to be a good year, and I was able to manage 54 engagements, a slight increase. Apart from the usual fixtures I met up with the owner of a group of garden centres who thought that a weekend visit from *Ceōl* would boost trade. These bookings were easy, with visits to Aylesbury and Burnham Beeches in Buckinghamshire, and Handcross and Chichester in Sussex, spread over two weekends in October. I found that at these events I was playing to a completely new public, many of them who had never seen a fair organ. Obviously they didn't attend county shows, rallies, or live in the towns where I made street collections. But, as always, I found an enthusiastic audience.

At Easter I had gone to Bridport Place in north London at the invitation of the Shoreditch Community Centre. It seemed a strange location for a fair organ but the event was well organised and attracted a good crowd of Easter revellers. Trouble? Not on your life!

I felt particularly sad as I did the Carol Festival at Halesworth in Suffolk, although I was not then aware it was to be my last.

WITH THE NEXT season came the sickening awareness that I would soon have to advertise *Ceōl*. I had 40 bookings and I determined to make a start on them and sell during the season: I would rather part with *Ceōl* while she was singing than when she was locked up and silent for the winter. I had no yard now, as the Old Road Paint Works was just a memory, and I didn't want to encourage the timewasters.

I covered Southend-on-Sea, Watford, Shoreditch again, and decided I could manage the Shropshire County Show one more time. It was at Shrewsbury that I first let it be known that *Ceōl* was for sale, and an old friend who had a small fair said he was interested. It was too sudden, and I dithered. Was that how I would react when the parting really came?

By the time I went to the Sellindge Steam Rally in Kent in late May, *Ceōl* was advertised in *World's Fair*, and the news had spread like wildfire around the rally field. On this, my last visit with the organ, I was sited next to my boyhood first love, the Burrell showman's engine *General Gough*, still the beautiful leviathan that she had been in the twenties.

I wondered how much time, money, labour and love had been spent in restoring her to such magnificence, and I found myself wishing I was a lad again. My old pal Smokey Shepherd was driving her and when he let me up onto the footplate I couldn't help saying: "It's taken me sixty-five years to get here." It was a boyhood dream realised at last.

From Sellindge I went to Rochester for a one-day recital as part of the Dickens Week, and when I arrived back home I had a lot of letters to read and phone calls to make. I was dead tired and decided to leave them all until the next day.

But the phone rang. As I was alone in the house I answered it.

"Is that Leonard Brooks? Tom Atkinson here. About that organ of yours; I'm very interested. Can you bring it over and let me see it?"

"Give me a ring tomorrow; I've just got home from Kent."

"Surely you know I live only just a little way down the road. Why don't you come over now?" Tom sounded totally sincere, and nothing like a timewaster, and he had the right idea about buying something unique: be persistent. When he told me he lived at Ingatestone, just ten miles away, I found I couldn't resist.

Meeting Tom Atkinson was not only a pleasure, it was a revelation. I had heard of him on a number of occasions but this was my first view of his collection and I soon realised he was a preservationist in every sense of the word. Standing in his garage was a magnificent 1926 20hp Rolls Royce in its original black paintwork. Before I could recover from that he took me to a barn and said: "How about this, then?"

Leonard hands over 'Ceōl' to Tom Atkinson in 1985.

'This' was only a 1912 Renault AX two-cylinder car in perfect condition. "Jump in."

I didn't actually jump. As I climbed carefully aboard, Tom cranked the motor and drove out of the gateway and down the country lane. The engine responded perfectly, and it was a wonderful experience to be sitting so high and able to look over the hedgerows. As he drove, Tom told me he had taken the car abroad several times, and it was a major attraction in France.

Back at the old farm Tom showed me his other possessions, including an early petrol pump. And then he took me to see his collection of organs. The first was a small street organ carrying the name of Keith Prowse and made by Victor Chiappa many, many years ago. There was a barrel organ of the type that Chiappa used to rent out by the day, and a 20 keyless Dean organ.

I could see that *Ceōl* would be quite at home here, and I knew that I was facing one of the great decisions of my life. Then it was my turn to show him *Ceōl*, and I played the first tune that Tommy Redburn had played for me when I bought the organ, *The Poet and the Peasant*. Afterwards, we talked, as I put off the moment of final commitment.

Tom added the inducement that settled it. "Leonard, I can see you'll have to be weaned away from *Ceōl*. I'll make you an offer and a promise: you can complete your bookings, and after that you can come out with her any time you wish. How's that?"

I knew I would never get a better offer, and *Ceōl*'s new home would be only ten miles away. We shook hands on the deal, and my dear friend had a new owner: the tears stung the back of my eyes. We agreed to have the official handing-over ceremony at Chelmsford Fête on 15 August, almost three months away.

Before those three months passed, I had to go back to the optician for a check-up, and he advised me to go to hospital at once. In addition to my original trouble, I now had glaucoma.

And it was at that hospital that the doctor certified that I was no longer fit to drive. My eyes were just about good enough for me to see on his desk the form which would deprive me of my driving licence.

So I would never again drive the Transit, never again take *Ceōl* to an event on my own. But it was not to be the end of my travels as Dee, Tom, or Tom's friend Roger Booty took over the driving.

I managed to fulfil all the bookings, including the two-day Henham Rally in Suffolk and the two-day Hadlow Down Organ Festival the following week.

Ceōl spent that winter in Tom's barn with his other trophies and Dee and I sold our home in the London suburbs to move to somewhere quieter; we chose a bungalow near Frinton-on-Sea in Essex, ironically one of the few places in the county where I had never played *Ceōl*. The following year, my last, had a mere 22 bookings, nine of them street collections and only two of them rallies: the mad, mad scene at Henham Hall, and the prestigious affair at Hadlow Down. It was the perfect event on which to close my years on the road.

We arrived on site in mid-morning, and nothing appeared to have changed since the previous year. Peter Haining directed us to my old site, a gesture that we appreciated. We drove down to the lower meadow past a line of sizzling steam rollers and traction engines and reversed into our place near the workshop yard, where we had access to power.

I took the first stint at the keyframe and noted the organ was in good voice thanks to its winter overhaul by John Page who had taken over after Victor Chiappa retired. I noticed there were many more books added to the plentiful supply I had had, probably enough for eight hours' playing time, but there was that extra weight and space problem.

When Tom came to take over, he said: "Off you go, Len, and meet your pals. Take all the time you want."

The first friend I met was Norman Hobbs, owner of three good organs including a Mortier, but he hadn't brought that one to the rally. I looked for Claude Jessett, an extremely modest man who had done much for preservation but I learned that he had recently died. Fittingly, one of his traction engines joined the funeral procession.

Mrs Jessett was at the rally, and she confirmed she was keeping her husband's interests alive; she had three organs and a steam roller as well as the traction engine, and she was engaged in organising two rallies. And all I did was take one organ and two traction engines around the country!

Neither was the *Southern Queen* on site. She had often stood by *Ceōl* at Hadlow Down but she was at the boilermakers for a new fire box. Her driver Owen was to die soon after, and he would be laid to rest beside Claude in the same churchyard.

I went past the rows of traders' stalls and soon found my old friend Arthur Mantle with his 38-key Bursens, of which only two were built. Next, a look at Ron Armstrong's collection of phonographs and other recording apparatus, dating back to the nineteenth century. Ron tours with a 35-key Limonaire, an organ built in 1910 and which once graced a cakewalk.

Soon I was looking at some of Mrs Jessett's organs including the *Silver Cherub*, a Limonaire built in Paris in 1910. It served on roundabouts in France and Belgium until 1939 and its proprietor was sent to a concentration camp from which he never returned.

The *Nightingale of the Wood* was a 52-keyless Ruth built in 1900 which travelled the fairs and wine festivals of the Black Forest until the outbreak of war; it reappeared in 1970 having been rebuilt by a Cornish lighthouse keeper, and it joined Claude's collection in 1974. Finally there was *Rainbow*, an 88-keyless dance organ built by Arthur Bursens of Antwerp which travelled the fairs before being installed in a dance hall. Damaged by the occupying Germans, Bursens rebuilt it and it made its first appearance at Hadlow Down in 1966.

My tour of reverie took me to the beautifully-restored Burrell 6hp showman's road locomotive *St Breannock*, which I had last seen in the North Country. I made a last call at Les Parsons's great Meccano emporium, a fascinating collection of working fairground items which included an organ that ran cards through its keyframe. I had intended to see Doug and Anne Hooker's Dean organ *Blossom*, but time beat me and I made my way back to *Ceōl* only an hour or so before we were due to pack up. My rally days were over.

BUT NOT MY collecting days; there were to be four more before my final collection in Shenfield, Brentwood. You will know from reading my story that I enjoyed *almost* every minute of my travels with *Firefly, Prince* and *Ceōl*, but the greatest satisfaction came from helping others less fortunate than us. Before my failing sight took me off the road, we had passed the £120,000 mark and, as I write, I know that *Ceōl* and Tom Atkinson have added considerably to that total, with £250,000 as the combined target. I find this the most satisfying tribute to my life as Mister Organ Man. What do you think?

1972

Date	Place	County	Event
Apr 28-29	Walpole St Andrew	Norf	Rally
May 5	Medway (Chatham)	Kent	Rally
Jun 4	Thurrock	Essex	Town Show
Jul 1-2	Gt Missenden	Bucks	Rally
Jul 8-9	Dagenham	Essex	Town Show
Jul 14-16	Knebworth House	Bucks	Rally
Jul 29-30	Milton Keynes	Bucks	Town Show
Aug 5-6	Northampton	N'nts	Steam Show
Aug 12-13	Knowl Hill	Berks	Rally
Aug 26-27	Norwich	Norf	Rally

1973

Date	Place	County	Event
Mar 10	Romford	Essex	Street Collection
Apr 4	Harpenden	Herts	Fête
Apr 21	Watford	Herts	Street Collection
Apr 22-23	Hereford	Hfs & W	Rally
Apr 28-29	Merton (Wandle Pk)	London	Rally
May 5-6	Walpole St Andrew	Norf	Rally
May 6	St Bart's Hospital	London	Street Fair
May 19	Shenfield	Essex	Street Collection
May 26-27	Sellindge	Kent	Rally
Jun 2	Hadlow Down	Suss	Rally
Jun 9	Tiptree	Essex	Fête
Jun 16-17	Ripon	W.Yorks	Rally
Jun 20	Warley Hospital	Essex	Recital
Jun 23	Epsom	Surrey	Fête
Jun 24	Grays	Essex	Fête
Jul 2-12	Nuneaton	Warks	Ford Exhibition
Jul 13-15	Stratford-upon-Avon	Warks	Steam Show
Sep 9	Chelmsford	Essex	Rally
Sep 16	Roxton Park	Norf	Rally
Sep 21	Shenfield School	Essex	Recital
Sep 23	Hornchurch	Essex	Fête
Sep 30-31	Paddock Wood	Kent	Rally
Oct 6	Roding Valley	Essex	Firework Display
Oct 8	Hadlow Down	Kent	Rally
Oct 22	Sittingbourne	Kent	Light Railway
Oct 27-29	Sittingbourne	Kent	Steam & Fireworks
Nov 4	Doubtfires, York	Yks	Firework Display
Nov 25	Aspley Guise	Bucks	Street Collection

1974

Date	Place	County	Event
Mar 23	Dartford	Kent	Street Collection
Mar 24	Alexandra Palace	London	John Carter sale
Apr 13	Watford	Herts	Street Collection
Apr 20	Harpenden	Herts	Fête
Apr 27-28	Merton	London	Rally
May 4-5	Walpole St Andrew	Norf	Rally
May 11	Shenfield	Essex	Street Collection
May 18	Risley	Beds	Fête
May 25	Rainham	Kent	Town Spectacular
May 26-27	Sellindge	Kent	Rally
May 28	Heybridge	Essex	Sacha Distel Night
Jun 1-6	Blackbush	Hants	Rally
Jun 5-6	Chester	Ches	County Show
Jun 7	Millisle	Cumbria	Recital
Jun 8-9	Levens Hall	Cumbria	Rally
Jun 15-16	Aberdeen	Aberdeen	Rally
Jun ??	Ripon	W Yorks	Rally
Jun 22-23	Grays	Essex	Town Show
Jun 29-30	Netley Marsh	Hants	Rally
Jul 6-7	Peterborough	Cambs	Works Fête
Jul 20-22	Tewkesbury	Glos	Steam Show
Jul 28-29	Milton Keynes	Bucks	Town Show
Aug 4-5	Cromford	Derbys	Rally
Aug 11-12	Knowl Hill	Berks	Rally
Aug 13	Aldeburgh	Suff	Town Carnival
Aug 18-19	Caenby Corner	Lincs	Rally
Aug 25-27	Royal Showground	Warks	Rally
Sep 1-2	Hinckley	Leics	Rally
Sep 9	Horsham	Suss	Rally
Sep 15-16	Roxton Park	Beds	Rally
Sep 21-23	Stourpaine	Dorset	Rally
Sep 26-28	Liverpool	Mersey	Exhibition
Sep 29-30	Paddock Wood	Kent	Rally
Oct 6	Beaulieu	Hants	Steam Show
Oct 21	Sittingbourne	Kent	Light Railway
Nov 10	Hornchurch	Essex	Bazaar
Nov 24	Watford	Herts	Street Collection
Jul 13-14	Dagenham	Essex	Town Show
Jul 20-21	John Carter's	Berks	Steam Show
Jul 27-28	Brixton	London	Town & Country
Aug 3-4	Cromford	Derbys	Rally
Aug 10-11	Castle Howard	N Yorks	Rally
Aug 17-18	Caenby Corner	Lincs	Rally
Aug 24-26	Royal Showground	Warks	Rally
Aug 30-1	Sharnforth	Leics	Rally
Sep 7-8	Milton Keynes	Bucks	Town Show
Sep 14-15	Roxton Park	Beds	Rally
Sep 21-22	Stourpaine	Dorset	Rally
Sep 28-29	Tonbridge	Kent	Rally
Oct 5-6	Beaulieu	Hants	Rally
Oct 12-13	Hadlow Down	Sussex	Rally
Oct 19	Sittingbourne	Kent	Light Railway
Oct 20	Alexandra Palace	London	Vintage Sale
Nov 2	Olney	Bucks	Phil Ives
Nov 9	Hornchurch	Essex	Charity Sale
Nov 16	Romford	Essex	Street Collection
Nov 23	Watford	Herts	Street Collection
Dec 12	Harold Wood	Essex	Recital

1975

Date	Place	County	Event
Feb 22	Harlow	Essex	Street Collection
Mar 30	Sittingbourne	Kent	Light Railway
Apr 11	Chelmsford	Essex	Street Collection
Apr 12	Harpenden	Herts	Children's Home
Apr 13	Alexandra Palace	London	John Carter Sale
Apr 26-27	Merton	London	Rally
May 4-5	Walpole St Andrew	Norf	Rally
May 18	Oldchurch Hospital	Essex	Fête
May 24-26	Sellindge	Kent	Rally
May 28-29	Stafford	Staffs	County Show
May 31	Harlow	Essex	Street Collection
Jun 7	Southend-on-Sea	Essex	Street Collection
Jun 14-16	Bacton	Suff	Rally
Jun 21	Tiptree	Essex	Fête
Jun 22	Grays	Essex	Town Show
Jun 28	Harlow Old Town	Essex	Steam Show
Jun 29	Chigwell	Essex	Vintage Car Show
Jul 5-6	Ardingly	Suss	Rally
Jul 12-13	Dagenham	Essex	Town Show
Jul 17	Billericay	Essex	Street Collection
Jul 20-21	Polegate	Sussex	Rally
Aug 9	Billericay	Essex	Fête
Aug 16-17	Caenby Corner	Lincs	Rally
Aug 23-25	Royal Showground	Warks	Rally
Sep 6-7	Leigh-on-Sea	Essex	Regatta
Sep 13-14	Roxton Park	Beds	Rally
Sep 20	Coxtie Gr.	Essex	Fête
Oct 4-5	Beaulieu	Hants	Rally
Oct 10	Sharnbrook	Beds	Firework Night
Oct 11-12	Hadlow Down	Suss	Rally
Oct 19	Sittingbourne	Kent	Light Railway
Oct 26	Alexandra Palace	London	John Carter Sale
Nov 8	Olney	Bucks	Phil Ives
Dec 17	Harold Wood	Essex	Recital

1976

Date	Place	County	Event
Mar 6	Chelmsford	Essex	Street Collection
Apr 17	Harpenden	Herts	Children's Home
Apr 18-19	Sittingbourne	Kent	Easter Railway
May 1-2	Walpole St Andrew	Norf	Rally
May 8	Southend-on-Sea	Essex	Shelford House
May 15	Romford	Essex	Fête
May 19-20	Shrewsbury	Salop	County Show
May 22	Brentwood	Essex	Street Collection
May 29-31	Sellindge	Kent	Rally
Jun 1	Colchester	Essex	Recital
Jun 2-3	Ipswich	Suff	County Show
Jun 5	Tiptree	Essex	Fête
Jun 12	Hawkeswell	Essex	Fête
Jun 13	Burnham Beeches	Bucks	Rally
Jun 18	Gt Leighs,	Essex	County Show
Jun 19	Rainham	Kent	Town Spectacular
Jun 20	Chigwell	Essex	Vintage Car Show
Jun 23	Romford	Essex	Street Collection
Jun 26-27	Little Houghton	N'hants	Flower Show
Jul 3	Dagenham	Essex	Fête
Jul 4	Ardingly	Sussex	Rally
Jul 10-11	Dagenham	Essex	Town Show
Jul 17	Chigwell	Essex	Fête
Jul 18	Windsor Forest	Berks	Rally
Jul 24	North Weald	Essex	Fête
Jul 25	Cambridge	Cambs	Pump Station Museum
Aug 7-8	Ashford	Kent	Fête
Aug 14-15	Knowl Hill	Berks	Rally
Aug 21-22	Reading	Berks	Rally
Aug 23	Aldeburgh	Suff	Carnival
Aug 28-30	Royal Showground	Warks	Rally
Sep 4	Bungay	Suff	Bun Feast
Sep 5	Alexandra Palace	London	Vintage Sale
Sep 10	Rayleigh	Essex	Windmill Fête
Sep 11	Billericay	Essex	Street Collection
Sep 12	Leigh-on-Sea	Essex	Regatta
Sep 18	Kelvedon	Essex	Fête
Sep 25-26	Henham	Suff	Rally
Oct 2-3	Hadlow Down	Suss	Rally
Oct 7	Sharnbrook	Beds	Firework Night
Oct 9	Chelmsford	Essex	Street Collection
Oct 16	Wokingham	Berks	Steam Show
Oct 17	Sittingbourne	Kent	Light Railway
Oct 30	Olney	Bucks	Phil Ives Fireworks
Nov 5-6	Beaulieu	Hants	Rally & Bonfire
Nov 20	Watford	Herts	Street Collection
Nov 21	Colchester	Essex	Recital
Dec 15	Romford	Essex	Recital

1977

Date	Place	County	Event
Mar 12	Chelmsford	Essex	Street Collection
Apr 9-11	Cider Brewery	Hfs & W	Rally
Apr 16	Colchester	Essex	Street Collection
May 1	Walpole St Andrew	Norf	Rally
May 5	Halstead	Essex	Street Collection
May 14-15	Stoke Goldington	Bucks	Rally
May 18-19	Shrewsbury	Salop	County Show
May 21	Watford	Herts	Street Collection
Jun 1-2	Ipswich	Suff	County Show
Jun 5	Sellindge	Kent	Rally
Jun 7	Sharnbrook	Beds	Jubilee Day
Jun 11-12	Epsom	Surr	Rally
Jun 17-18	Gt Leighs	Essex	County Show
Jun 24-25	Ashford	Kent	Town Show
Jun 30	Goxtie Green	Essex	Programme Sales
Jul 1	Mildenhall	Suff	Advertising Recital

Date	Place	County	Event
Jul 2	Coxtie Green	Essex	Fête
Jul 7	Halstead	Essex	School Fête
Jul 9-10	Dagenham	Essex	Town Show
Jul 13	Runwell Hospital	Essex	Fête
Jul 17	Weeting	Suff	Rally
Jul 27	Clacton-on-Sea	Essex	Fête
Jul 30-31	Polegate	Suss	Rally
Aug 6	Southend-on-Sea	Essex	Street Collection
Aug 7	Holton	Oxon	Rally
Aug 13	Ipswich	Suff	Carnival
Aug 14	Southend-on-Sea	Essex	Fête
Aug 15	Aldeburgh	Suff	Carnival
Aug 20-21	Fairford	Glos	Rally
Aug 27-29	Harlow	Essex	Town Show
Aug 30	Leicester	Leics	Town Show
Sep 4	John Carter	Berks	Steam Show
Sep 18	Roxton Park	Beds	Rally
Sep 24-25	Henham	Suff	Rally
Oct 1-2	Hadlow Down	Suss	Rally
Oct 11	Doddinghurst	Essex	Recording Session
Oct 16	Sittingbourne	Kent	Light Railway
Oct 29	Olney	Bucks	Phil Ives Fireworks
Nov 5	Beaulieu	Hants	Firework Night
Dec 14	Runwell Hospital	Essex	Carol Service
Dec 16	Borehamwood	Herts	Recital
Dec 17	Billericay	Essex	Street Collection
Dec 18	Canewdon	Essex	Recital
Dec 26	Sittingbourne	Kent	Christmas Steam-Up

1978

Date	Place	County	Event
Mar 11	Chelmsford	Essex	Street Collection
Mar 23-27	Southport	Lancs	Model Exhibition
Apr 30-1	Hereford	Hfs & W	GWR Steam Show
May 10-11	Ardingly	Suss	County Show
May 12	Braintree	Essex	Street Collection
May 13-15	Stoke Goldington	Bucks	Rally
May 17-18	Shrewsbury	Salop	County Show
May 19	Telford	Salop	Recital
May 20	Hitchin	Herts	Recital
May 21	S. Woodham Ferrers	Essex	Rally
May 29	Sharnbrook	Beds	Street Fête
May 30-1	Ipswich	Suff	County Show
Jun 3-4	Hadlow Down	Suss	Rally
Jun 10-11	Holton	Oxon	Rally
Jun 14	Runwell Hospital	Essex	Fête
Jun 16	Cuddesdon	Oxon	College Party
Jun 17-18	Andover	Hants	Rally
Jun 24-25	Ashford	Kent	County Show
Jun 28	Royal Free Hospital	London	Recital
Jun 30-2	Newport	Gwent	Wales & West Show
Jul 4	St Albans	Herts	Hospital Recital
Jul 7	Mildenhall	Suff	Carnival
Jul 8	Harlow	Essex	Street Collection
Jul 9	Dagenham	Essex	Town Show
Jul 13-15	Detling	Kent	County Show
Jul 16	Milton Keynes	Bucks	Bow Brickhill Fête
Jul 24-26	Clacton-on-Sea	Essex	Fête
Aug 1	Toothill	Essex	Event Promotion
Aug 6	Newbury	Berks	John Carter Show
Aug 11	Blackmore	Essex	Village Show
Aug 16	Knowl Hill	Berks	Rally
Aug 18	St Ives	Cwl	Publicity Recital
Aug 19-20	Camborne	Cwl	W. of England Rally
Aug 21	Aldeburgh	Suff	Carnival
Aug 26-27	Harlow	Essex	Town Show
Aug 28-29	Leicester	Leics	County Show
Sep 2	Leigh-on-Sea	Essex	Regatta
Sep 3	Booker	Bucks	John Carter Airshow
Sep 10	Gaddesdon Row	Herts	Rally
Sep 17	Roxton Park	Beds	Rally
Sep 23-24	Henham	Suff	Rally
Sep 30-1	Hadlow Down	Suss	Rally
Oct 6-12	Brean Sands	Avon	Model Exhibition
Oct 15	Sittingbourne	Kent	Light Railway
Oct 28	Olney	Bucks	Phil Ives Fireworks
Nov 4	Beaulieu	Hants	Firework Party
Dec 10	Colchester	Essex	Recital, Mental Home
Dec 20	Runwell Hospital	Essex	Recital
Dec 24	Henley on Thames	Oxon	Recital

1979

Date	Place	County	Event
Mar 3	Chelmsford	Essex	Street Collection
Apr 14-16	Barrow-in-Furness	Cumb	Model Exhibition
Apr 28	Hockley	Essex	Fête
May 5	Walpole St Andrew	Norf	Rally
May 12	Amersham	Bucks	Street Collection
May 13	Stoke Goldington	Bucks	Rally
May 16-17	Shrewsbury	Salop	County Show
May 19-20	Moulton	Lincs	Show & Fête
May 27	Welford	Leics	Rally
May 28	Shrewsbury	Salop	Recital
Jun 1	Billericay	Essex	Fête
Jun 2	Dartford	Kent	Fête
Jun 3	Hadlow Down	Suss	Rally
Jun 9	Colchester	Essex	Fête & Recital
Jun 10	Rochford	Essex	Fête
Jun 11	Maldon	Essex	Street Collection
Jun 11	Bicnacre	Essex	Birthday Party
Jun 14	Oxted	Surr	Street Collection
Jun 15	East Grinstead	Suss	Street Collection
Jun 16	Lingfield	Surr	Fête
Jun 23	Maidstone	Kent	Fête
Jun 29	Mildenhall	Suff	Advertising Recital
Jul 7	Rochford	Essex	Fête
Jul 8	Ardingly	Suss	Rally
Jul 12-13	Detling	Kent	County Show
Jul 14-15	Halesworth	Suff	Fête

Jul	21	Southend-on-Sea	Essex	Street Collection
Jul	23-25	Clacton-on-Sea	Essex	Collection & Fête
Jul	28-29	Polegate	Suss	Rally
Jul	31	Toothill	Essex	Advertising Recital
Aug	4	Tower of London	London	Street Collection
Aug	5	Oakham	Leics	County Show
Aug	11-12	Knowl Hill	Berks	Rally
Aug	16	Blackmore	Essex	Village Show
Aug	19	Brands Hatch	Kent	Rally
Aug	20	Aldeburgh	Suff	Carnival
Aug	25-28	Harlow	Essex	Town Show
Aug	28-29	Leicester	Leics	City Show
Aug	30	Swaffham	Norf	Recital
Sep	1	Dovercourt	Essex	Fête

Sep	2	Swaffham	Norf	Fête
Sep	9	Leigh-on-Sea	Essex	Regatta
Sep	16	North Weald	Essex	Epping Forest Show
Sep	19	Chatham	Kent	MacKays Recital
Sep	22-23	Henham	Suff	Rally
Sep	26	Chatham	Kent	MacKays Recital
Sep	29-5	Brean Sands	Avon	Model Exhibition
Oct	10	Stanmore	London	Steam-Up
Oct	27	Olney	Bucks	Phil Ives
Nov	3	Beaulieu	Hants	Firework Party
Dec	5	St Katherine's Dock	London	Trade Show
Dec	9	Colchester	Essex	Recital
Dec	17	Runwell Hospital	Essex	Recital

1980

Mar	3	Basildon	Essex	Street Collection
Mar	9	Great Baddow	Essex	Marconi Sports
Apr	5-7	Watford	Herts	Leisure Centre
May	5	Rayleigh	Essex	Windmill Fête
May	10-11	Stoke Goldington	Bucks	Rally
May	16	Braintree	Essex	Street Collection
May	17	Westerham	Kent	Programme Sales
May	18	Sittingbourne	Kent	Light Railway
May	21-22	Shrewsbury	Salop	County Show
May	24	Barnet	London	Programme Sales
May	25-26	Welford	N'hnts	Rally
May	28-29	Ipswich	Suff	County Show
Jun	1	Cotton	Suff	Rally
Jun	6	Dartford	Kent	Street Collection
Jun	7	Dartford	Kent	Fête
Jun	8	Rochford	Essex	Fête
Jun	14	Beckenham	Kent	Fête
Jun	16	Oxted	Surr	Street Collection
Jun	17	Edenbridge	Kent	Street Collection
Jun	19	Caterham	Kent	Street Collection
Jun	20	Crawley	Suss	Street Collection
Jun	20	Cuddesdon	Oxon	End of Term Party
Jun	21	Lingfield	Surr	School Fête
Jun	26	Southend-on-Sea	Essex	Hospital Recital
Jun	27	Hockley	Essex	Recital
Jun	28	Harlow	Essex	Street Collection
Jul	5	Southend-on-Sea	Essex	Street Collection
Jul	6	Ardingly	Suss	Rally

Jul	10-12	Detling	Kent	County Show
Jul	13	Dagenham	Essex	Town Show
Jul	19	Galleywood	Essex	Programme Sales
Jul	20	Brixton	London	Town & Country Show
Jul	26-30	Clacton-on-Sea	Essex	Carnival
Aug	2-3	Biggleswade	Beds	County Festival
Aug	9-10	Knowl Hill	Berks	Rally
Aug	18	Aldeburgh	Suff	Carnival
Aug	19	Southend-on-Sea	Essex	Hospital Recital
Aug	23-25	Stoneleigh	Warks	Rally
Aug	26	Leicester	Leics	City Show
Aug	28	Watford	Herts	Childrens' Day
Aug	30-31	Blenheim Palace	Oxon	Rally
Sep	6	Leigh-on-Sea	Essex	Regatta
Sep	7	Wooton	Suff	Fête
Sep	12	Brent	London	Show
Sep	13	Westminster	London	GLC Celebration
Sep	14	Brent	London	Show
Sep	20-21	Henham	Suff	Rally
Sep	27-29	Hadlow Down	Suss	Rally
Oct	4-5	New Romney	Kent	Light Railway
Oct	6-10	Brean Down	Avon	Model Exhibition
Oct	19	Sittingbourne	Kent	Light Railway
Nov	1	Beaulieu	Hants	Firework Night
Dec	12	Bethnal Green	London	School Recital
Dec	14	Colchester	Essex	Recital
Dec	18	Runwell Hospital	Essex	Recital
Dec	23	Dartford	Kent	Street Collection

1981

Apr	20	Sittingbourne	Kent	Light Railway
May	3-4	Walpole St Andrew	Norf	Rally
May	9-10	Stoke Goldington	Bucks	Rally
May	15	Braintree	Essex	Street Collection
May	16	Westerham	Kent	Programme Sales
May	17	Sittingbourne	Kent	Railway Special Day
May	20-21	Shrewsbury	Salop	County Show
May	23-24	Welford	N'hnts	Rally

May	28	Dartford	Kent	Fête
May	30	Royston	Herts	Rose Fair
May	31	Rochford	Essex	Fête
Jun	6-7	Milton Keynes	Bucks	Town Show
Jun	13	Lingfield	Surr	School Fête
Jun	26	Chelmsford	Essex	Programme Sales
Jul	3	Newton Abbot	Devon	End of Term Party
Jul	5	Eltham	London	Fête

Jul 11	Brentwood	Essex	Programme Sales
Jul 12	Temple Mills	London	Rly Works Open Day
Jul 13	Dagenham	Essex	Town Show
Jul 16-17	Detling	Kent	County Show
Jul 18	Southend-on-Sea	Essex	Fête
Jul 25-29	Clacton-on-Sea	Essex	Fête
Aug 1	Great Bentley	Essex	Fête
Aug 2	Great Leighs	Essex	Fête
Aug 22-23	Rochford	Essex	Fête
Aug 26	Clacton-on-Sea	Essex	Fête
Aug 28-29	Stoneleigh	Warks	Rally
Aug 30-31	Leicester	Leics	Town Show
Sep 3	Watford	Herts	Recital
Sep 5	Colchester	Essex	Street Collection
Sep 6	Brands Hatch	Kent	Rally
Sep 13	Leigh-on-Sea	Essex	Regatta
Sep 18	Beccles	Suff	Advertising Recital
Sep 19-20	Henham	Suff	Rally
Sep 26-27	Hadlow Down	Suss	Organ Festival
Oct 2	Folkestone	Kent	Advertising Recital
Oct 3-4	New Romney	Kent	Light Railway
Oct 17-18	Sittingbourne	Kent	Light Railway
Oct 31-1	Beaulieu	Hants	Rally & Fireworks
Dec 5	Southwold	Suff	Switch on Christmas lights

1982

Jan 23	Southend-on-Sea	Essex	Street Collection
Apr 12	Islington	London	Easter Fair
May 3	Rayleigh	Essex	Windmill Fair
May 8-9	Stoke Goldington	Bucks	Rally
May 19-20	Shrewsbury	Salop	County Show
May 22-23	Cubbington	Warks	Fête
May 30-31	Sellindge	Kent	Rally
Jun 2-3	Ipswich	Suff	County Show
Jun 5	Basildon	Essex	Street Collection
Jun 6	Runwell Hospital	Essex	Fête
Jun 12	Lingfield	Surr	School Fête
Jun 13	Merton	London	Rally
Jun 20	Dagenham	Essex	Ford Sports Day
Jun 24	Hythe	Kent	Light Rly
Jun 26-27	New Romney	Kent	Rally
Jun 30	Rayleigh	Essex	Publicity Rally
Jul 10	ıthend-on-Sea	Essex	Shalford House Fête
Jul 11	Dagenham	Essex	Town Show
Jul 15-17	Detling	Kent	County Show
Jul 18	Lingfield	Surr	Racecourse Show
Jul 24-28	Clacton-on-Sea	Essex	Fundraising Fête
Jul 25	Framlingham	Suff	Rally
Aug 1	Palmers Green	London	Sports Day
Aug 14-15	Knowl Hill	Berks	Rally
Aug 21-22	Glastonbury	Som	Childrens World
Aug 25-26	Bristol Docks	Avon	Childrens Show
Aug 28-30	Stoneleigh	Warks	Rally
Aug 31	Leicester	Leics	Town Show
Sep 1-2	Watford	Herts	Rally
Sep 4-5	Leigh-on-Sea	Essex	Regatta
Sep 12	Chelmsford	Essex	Cramphorns Fête
Sep 15	Lowestoft	Suff	Publicity Rally
Sep 17	Beccles	Suff	Publicity Rally
Sep 18-19	Henham	Suff	Rally
Sep 25-26	Hadlow Down	Suss	Organ Festival
Oct 2	Stanmore	London	Steam-Up
Oct 3	Brentwood	Essex	Hotel Exhibition
Dec 27	Henley-on-Thames	Oxon	Carol Recital

1983

Mar 26	Chelmsford	Essex	Street Collection
Apr 4	Islington	London	Easter Show
May 2	Rayleigh	Essex	Windmill Fair
May 7	Billericay	Essex	Street Collection
May 14-15	Stoke Goldington	Bucks	Rally
May 18-19	Shrewsbury	Salop	County Show
May 21-22	Rickmansworth	Herts	Football Show
May 28	Billericay	Essex	Street Collection
May 29-30	Sellindge	Kent	Rally
Jun 1-2	Rochester	Kent	Dickens Week
Jun 5	Hadlow Down	Suss	Rally
Jun 11	Lingfield	Surr	Fête
Jun 19	Colchester	Essex	Fun Run Day
Jul 2	Harlow	Essex	Street Collection
Jul 8	Brentwood	Essex	Programme Sales
Jul 9	Palmers Green	London	Fête
Jul 10	Rochford	Essex	Town Show
Jul 14-16	Detling	Kent	County Show
Jul 17	Harlow	Essex	Fête
Jul 23	Hastings	Suss	Programme Sales
Jul 27	Runwell Hospital	Essex	Fête
Jul 30	Watford	Herts	Street Collection
Jul 31	Lingfield	Surr	Racecourse Show
Aug 13-14	Knowl Hill	Berks	Rally
Aug 29-30	Leicester	Leics	Town Show
Sep 11	Leigh-on-Sea	Essex	Regatta
Sep 13	Lowestoft	Suff	Advertising
Sep 16	Beccles	Suff	Recital
Sep 17-18	Henham	Suff	Rally
Sep 24-25	Hadlow Down	Suss	Rally
Oct 1	St Bart's Hospital	London	Street Fair
Nov 9	Beaulieu	Hants	Firework Night
Nov 12	Colchester	Essex	Street Collection
Nov 14	Wickford	Essex	Christmas Bazaar

1984

Jan 28	Southend-on-Sea	Essex	Street Collection
Apr 7	Bicnacre	Essex	Fête
Apr 23	Islington	London	Easter Fair
May 5	Springfield	Essex	Fête
May 7	Rayleigh	Essex	Windmill Fair
May 11	Braintree	Essex	Programme Sales
May 16-17	Shrewsbury	Salop	County Show
May 19	Watford	Herts	Street Collection
May 26-27	Stoke Goldington	Bucks	Rally
Jun 3	Hadlow Down	Suss	Rally
Jun 7	Guys Hospital	London	Fête
Jun 16	Crawley	Suss	Street Collection
Jun 19	Lingfield	Surr	Racecourse Rally
Jun 30	Harlow	Essex	Street Collection
Jul 2	Ongar	Essex	Advertising Fête
Jul 8	Rochford	Essex	Fête
Jul 10	Ongar	Essex	Advertising Recital
Jul 12-15	Detling	Kent	County Show
Jul 16	Standon Massey	Essex	Fête
Jul 21	Folkestone	Kent	Street Collection
Jul 28	Sudbury	Suff	Advertising
Aug 2	Brandon	Suff	Recital
Aug 4-5	Elstow	Beds	Rally
Aug 11-12	Knowl Hill	Berks	Rally
Aug 25	Rayleigh	Essex	Street Collection
Aug 27-28	Leicester	Leics	Town Show
Aug 31	Burnham Beeches	Bucks	Street Collection
Sep 9	Leigh-on-Sea	Essex	Regatta
Sep 12	Darenth	Kent	Hospital Fête
Sep 20	Lowestoft	Suff	Advertising
Sep 21	Beccles	Suff	Recital
Sep 22-23	Henham	Suff	Rally
Sep 29-30	Hadlow Down	Suss	Festival
Oct 6	Chelmsford	Essex	Street Collection
Oct 20	Aylesbury	Bucks	⎫
Oct 20	Burnham Beeches	Bucks	⎬ Garden Centre
Oct 27	Hand Cross	Suss	⎭ Fête
Oct 28	Chichester	Suss	
Nov 3	Beaulieu	Hants	Firework Night
Nov 10	Wickford	Essex	Christmas Bazaar
Nov 17	Ipswich	Suff	Street Collection
Dec 14	Halesworth	Suff	Carol Recital

1985

Jan 26	Southend-on-Sea	Essex	Street Collection
Apr 15	Islington	London	Easter Fair
May 4	Springfield	Essex	School Recital
May 6	Rayleigh	Essex	Windmill Fair
May 15-16	Shrewsbury	Salop	County Show
May 18	Rickmansworth	Herts	Fête
May 25-27	Sellindge	Kent	Rally
May 31	Rochester	Kent	Hotel Recital
Jun 1	Basildon	Essex	Street Collection
Jun 2	Hadlow Down	Suss	Recital
Jun 14	Haywards Heath	Suss	Street Collection
Jun 15	Lingfield	Surr	Fête
Jul 13	Rochford	Essex	Fête
Jul 27	Ashampstead	Berks	Street Fair
Aug 3	Southend-on-Sea	Essex	Street Collection
Aug 10-11	Knowl Hill	Berks	Rally
Aug 26	Chelmsford	Essex	Fête
Sep 1	Leigh-on-Sea	Essex	Regatta
Sep 7	Southend-on-Sea	Essex	Street Collection
Sep 18	Lowestoft	Suff	Recital
Sep 20	Beccles	Suff	Recital
Sep 21-22	Henham	Suff	Rally
Sep 28-29	Hadlow Down	Suss	Organ Festival
Nov 9	Wickford	Essex	Christmas Bazaar

1986

Mar 15	Chelmsford	Essex	Street Collection
Mar 31	Islington	London	Easter Fair
May 5	Rayleigh	Essex	Windmill Fair
May 16	Braintree	Essex	Programme Sales
Jun 29	Cottered	Herts	Street Fair
Jul 12	Margaretting	Essex	Fête
Jul 18	Rochford	Essex	Fête
Jul 20	Moreton	Essex	Street Fair
Sep 6	Southend-on-Sea	Essex	Street Collection
Sep 7	Leigh-on-Sea	Essex	Regatta
Sep 17	Lowestoft	Suff	Advertising
Sep 19	Beccles	Suff	Recital
Sep 20-21	Henham	Suff	Rally
Sep 27-28	Hadlow Down	Suss	Rally
Oct 4	Chelmsford	Essex	Street Collection
Dec 13	Shenfield	Essex	Street Collection
Dec 20	Shenfield	Essex	Street Collection